Edgar Wallace, who wrote 170 novels as well as plays and short stories, including, of course, *King Kong*, spent part of 1893 as a builder's labourer in Clacton on Sea. His biographer, Neil Clark, wrote that Wallace told his landlady that he would be *"a great man one day"* and he was right, with his first novel published in 1905. According to the History of Clacton (published 1966 by Clacton Urban District Council), Wallace visited the Pavilion at the Pier Head where he saw *"a very good concert"* with *"the ocean roaring underneath"*.

Anna Maria Mackenzie (1760?-1816?): Other than several references to Anna being the daughter of an *"Essex coal merchant"* all that is known of her life is that she was widowed after giving birth to four children, which became the start of her career as an author. She wrote at least sixteen novels, probably more, because she used a variety of pseudonyms. These were mainly historical, some with Gothic elements, and can be found on internet sites that sell rare books. *Monmouth* – dated 1790 – seems to have received the most accolades, but she was able to earn a living from her writing, no mean feat in the 18th century. (ampltd.co.uk)

FAMOUS ESSEX AUTHORS

YOU HAVE NEVER HEARD OF

DEE GORDON

Essex Hundred Publications
Benfleet
Essex
www.essex100.com
ask@essex100.com

FAMOUS ESSEX AUTHORS
You have never heard of

This first edition published
February 2024
© Dee Gordon

All rights reserved.

No part of this book may be reprinted or reproduced or utilised
in any form or by any electronic, mechanical or other means,
now known or hereafter invented, including photocopying and
recording, or in any information storage or retrieval system,
without the permission in writing from the publishers.

A catalogue record for this book is available from
The British Library.
ISBN 9781739931629

Typeset by Hutchins Creative
Printed by 4edge Publishing.
22 Eldon Way
Eldon Way Industrial Estate
Hockley Essex SS5 4AD

Contents

Page No

7	List of Illustrations
9	Introduction
10	Acknowledgements
11	Dedication
12	**The Authors**
13	Douglas Adams
15	Margery Allingham
19	Sabine Baring-Gould
22	Nina Bawden
24	Arnold Bennett
27	Samuel Bensusan
30	Ursula Bloom
34	Robert Buchanan
37	Margaret Cavendish
40	Joseph Conrad
43	Warwick Deeping
46	Daniel Defoe
50	Henry de Vere Stacpoole
52	John Fowles
56	Margaret Gatty
58	Elinor Glyn
62	Eleanor Graham
64	James Hilton
67	Joseph Hocking
70	Sheila Holland
74	Fergus Hume
77	Harriett Jay
80	Sarah Kane
82	The Kernahans
85	Denise Levertov
87	William Morris
90	Arthur Morrison
93	Ruth Pitter
96	Francis Quarles

98	Roland Quittenton
100	Ruth Rendell
104	Dorothy Sayers
107	Dodie Smith
110	Susan Smythies
112	Joseph Strutt
114	The Taylors of Ongar
117	H.G.Wells
121	James Wentworth Day
122	R.D.Wingfield
125	Violet Winspear
128	William Winstanley
130	Mary Wollstonecraft
132	Lady Emma Caroline Wood
134	Lady Mary Wroth
136	**The Authors Who Did Not Quite Make the Essex list** – mainly because of short stays
139	**Poetic Licence** - well known figures with more tenuous links to Essex
143	**Essex Links to Classical Literature** - references to Essex in some of the classics
146	**More Literary Connections to Essex** – touches on playwrights, historians, and others connected to both writing and Essex
150	Conclusion
151	The Author, Dee Gordon
152	Essex Hundred Publications

List of Illustrations

Page No

13	Douglas Adams	Michael Hughes
15	Margery Allingham	Margery Allingham Society
19	Sabine Baring Gould	*Early Reminiscences* by S.Baring Gould
24	Arnold Bennett	Project Guttenberg Archive
27	Samuel Bensusan	Ann Puttock
30	Ursula Bloom	Ursula Bloom Literary Estate
37	Margaret Cavendish	Peter Lely in the Portland Collection
40	Joseph Conrad	Nat. Library of Poland, unknown author
43	Warwick Deeping	W.D. & H.O.Wills
46	Daniel Defoe	Wellcome Library
50	Henry de Vere Stacpoole	Walter Stoneman, Nat. Portrait Gallery
52	John Fowles	Ian M. Cook
56	Margaret Gatty	Mrs A. Gatty
58	Elinor Glyn	W.D. & H.O. Wills
64	James Hilton	James Hilton Society
67	Joseph Hocking	Mrs Galsworthy, Nat. Portrait Gallery
70	Sheila Holland	Jane Holland
74	Fergus Hume	Elliott & Fry
80	Sarah Kane	Aleks Sierz
82	Coulson Kernahan	Elliott & Fry
85	Denise Levertov	Bloodaxe Books
87	William Morris	Elliott & Fry
90	Arthur Morrison	*The Bookman*
93	Ruth Pitter	Enitharmon Press
96	Francis Quarles	Johnson
104	Dorothy L. Sayers	General Johnson Jameson
112	Joseph Strutt	John Ogborne
114	Jane and Ann Taylor	*Essex Review*
117	H.G.Wells	W.D.& H.O.Wills

List of Illustrations continued

122	R.D.Wingfield	Philip Wingfield
128	William Winstanley	Unknown Author
134	Lady Mary Wroth	John de Critz
137	Rebecca West	W.D.& H.O.Wills
138	Benjamin Disraeli	Stamina
139	Alfred Lord Tennyson	Mayall's
141	Edward Thomas	Arthur St. John Adcock
144	William Shakespeare	J.Salmon
149	Samuel Purchas	Richard Hakluyt

see inside back cover

Images within not credited are part of author or publisher collection. Every effort has been made to contact copyright holders of images reproduced in this book. If any have been inadvertently overlooked or incorrectly attributed the publisher and author will be pleased to make restitution at the earliest opportunity.

Introduction

This book has been a labour of love by someone who has written mainly local history up to this point, but *Famous Essex Authors You Have Never Heard Of* also encompasses a love of books, a fascination with writers, and a curiosity about celebrity culture and how it has evolved.

There are additional Essex authors who are not included, i.e. some of those who have written just one or two books (too many to list!) and those who are still writing, because information on the latter is likely to change even before this book is printed, e.g. Martina Cole or Richard Osman. There will be names that readers are familiar with, and many less familiar, and it is hoped that these less familiar works in particular will be sought out and brought back to life.

One of the joys of researching these talented people has been finding how under-valued Essex is as a cultural hub. The original idea focused on a dozen people, but the more research - over many years - the more authors kept popping up, with plenty of surprises. Who knew, for instance, that a working class girl from Dagenham (Sheila Holland) would become so successful as a romantic novelist under her various pseudonyms that she went into tax exile on a mansion on the Isle of Man, or that a quiet introvert from Leigh-on-Sea was capable of writing raunchy novels about Arab sheikhs although she had never travelled beyond England (Violet Winspear). Then there is the impressive R.D.Wingfield, whose books about Detective Frost were a huge favourite of the author, revealed as being from Basildon, not far from her own home in Southend.

Finding out why these people started writing, what motivated them, how they enjoyed success by using their lively imaginations, and how they sometimes struggled, has revealed a fascinating insight into the people of Essex. Even the 17th century aristocracy produced its memorable scribes with a Duchess from Colchester flaunting her exoticism and style with both the written and spoken word (Margaret Cavendish). It is hoped that readers will enjoy what is to come with just half the pleasure taken in its writing.

Peppered throughout these pages are boxes featuring additional relevant trivia which should hopefully extend readers' knowledge of Essex authors and their works. Enjoy!

Acknowledgements

The following are among those who have given invaluable support and assistance in varying degrees, all of which has been very welcome:

Ken Porter at Basildon Borough Heritage Group, Simon Donoghue at Havering Library Local Studies, Kate Pipe at Southend Forum, Teresa Trowers at Valence House Archive, Dagenham, Trevor and Judith Pound at the James Hilton Society, Ian Skillicorn at Wyndham Books, proof-readers Margaret Durkan and Phil Swain, Janet Phillips and members of Southend Scribes writers' group, author Stephen Nunn, Jane Holland, and Philip Wingfield.

To all writers everywhere, not just in Essex

THE AUTHORS

DOUGLAS ADAMS 1952-2001

Douglas Adams was born in Cambridge, but, at the age of five, his parents split up and his mother, Jan, a nurse, moved back in with her parents in Brentwood. His father remarried and moved to Stondon Massey, just a few miles away.

Adams was educated in Brentwood, firstly at Primrose Hill Primary, then at the renowned Brentwood Preparatory School, funded by his well-to-do stepmother. He seems to have preferred creative lessons to sporty ones which were perhaps the more obvious choice for someone of his height, and in fact never forgot receiving ten out of ten for a writing exercise. This was the only top score awarded by his teacher in their entire career!

When his mother re-married in 1964 and moved to Dorset, Adams switched from day boy to boarder after passing his eleven-plus with flying colours. On the strength of an essay discussing the Beatles alongside William Blake, he was awarded a place at St John's College, Cambridge to read English. He did not achieve his aim to join the famous Footlights society but managed a B.A. and M.A. in English Literature.

After graduation he spent several years contributing material to radio and television shows and revues. He also worked as a hospital porter, chicken shed cleaner, bodyguard, radio producer, and script editor of Doctor Who! *The Hitch Hiker's Guide to the Galaxy* (based on his experiences hitch-hiking in Europe) was aired in 1978 as a BBC Radio 4 series, giving little indication that it would prove a life-changing event – he was paid just £1,000. Six months later, he resigned to write the second radio series followed by the novel which went straight to Number

One in the UK Bestseller list. In 1984, he became the youngest author to be awarded a Golden Pen. Since then THGG has been a TV series, a record album, a computer game, and had several stage adaptations. Note that the number 42 (for those of you who have read the book...) could be attributed to his frequent visits as a child to the Chapel at Bradwell-on-Sea in Essex with its 42 panes of glass in each window!! Another Essex reference is in Chapter 9 of the book when the protagonists Arthur Dent and Ford Prefect remark that "everything looked a lot like the seafront at Southend" from the Starship Heart of Gold, although the sea was steady as a rock while the buildings washed up and down ... the resort being a place he would have visited.

Adams progressed with another six best selling novels in spite of his apparent inability to meet deadlines and his famed procrastination. He wrote several further novels as co-author. In all, he has sold at least 15 million books. Away from writing, he played guitar and collected left-handed guitars, and he was a campaigner for endangered species and embraced technology. (*Oxford Dictionary of National Biography* and *Hitchhiker, A Biography of Douglas Adams* by M.J.Simpson).

While living in Islington, London, in the 1980s, Adams made several trips to California to try and get THGG turned into a feature film, and in fact moved there in the 1990s after becoming a husband – in 1991 - and father. However, aged just forty-nine a sudden, unexpected heart attack while at the gym (in Santa Barbara, his last home) resulted in his untimely death, and his wife and daughter returned to the U.K.

His legacy, however, lives on, especially with regard to THGG. There are several appreciation societies, an annual Towel Day (May 25th), and, in 2005, the feature film finally appeared, with Martin Freeman as Arthur Dent, and featuring Warwick Davis plus the voices of Helen Mirren and Bill Bailey. The same year, an asteroid (number 25924) was named Douglas Adams in his memory. He would have been so proud!

Here's a quote from Adams that is particularly pertinent:

"The fact is I don't know where my ideas come from. Nor does any writer. The only real answer is to drink way too much coffee and buy yourself a desk that doesn't collapse when you beat your head against it." (www.goodreads.com)

MARGERY ALLINGHAM 1904-1966

Although Margery was born in West London, her family moved when she was five to the Old Rectory in Layer Breton, a remote village south west of Colchester on the edge of the Essex marshes. The eldest of three children, she was no doubt encouraged to write by her literary parents, both of whom wrote fiction for popular magazines and journals. In fact, it seems she was even allocated her own 'office' from the age of seven, at which time her father supervised her education when illness kept her from attending school regularly. She did, however, attend Endsleigh House School in Colchester from 1915 for three years, moving on to board at the Perse School for Girls in Cambridge and finally the Regent Street Polytechnic in London from 1921, where she studied speech and drama, enabling her to lose her childhood stammer.

Her first fee was for a story at the age of eight, published in one of her Aunt Maud's film journals, and she continued to write for her Aunt for many years. Her first novel *Blackkerchief Dick* appeared the year she left further education (1923). This novel was sub-titled *A Tale of Mersea Island*, a place she was familiar with as it had been the destination for family holidays, and there are many references to the River Blackwater and to the local marshes, known as historic smuggling haunts.

While at Regent Street Polytechnic she wrote a verse play, *Dido and Aeneas*, in which she played the leading role, and the art student who became her husband, Philip (Pip) Youngman Carter, designed the scenery. They married in 1927, but it was Margery who was the prime bread-winner until he started writing for *The Tatler* after World War II. Although unable to sell his art, he did help his wife by producing covers and illustrations for her works, and their marriage, while not perfect, lasted until her death.

Margery's family moved to the old Vicarage at Letheringham, near Framlingham in Suffolk, before her marriage, but she and Pip started married life in central London where she produced her first Albert Campion novels. In 1931 they moved to Viaduct Farm near Colchester, and then to D'Arcy house in Tolleshunt D'Arcy in 1937, just five miles from where she grew up. This was where she would spend the rest of her days, although she did retain a property in London.   .

Albert Campion, her famous detective, made his first appearance in 1929 in *The Crime at Black Dudley*. As a contemporary of Agatha Christie, Dorothy L. Sayers and Ngaio Marsh, Margery was at the forefront of the golden age of mystery writing, and she has also been regarded as matching P.G.Wodehouse for eccentricity and wit. She introduced a comic manservant for Campion in *Mystery Mile* (1930) but Campion himself is an enigmatic figure, languid and aristocratic. He proved her most successful creation, a creation which she developed in a series of novels, interrupted only by the Second World War.

She became involved in Air Raid Precautions work, served as First Aid Commandant for her district, and organised the billeting and care of evacuees from London. She was also set to function as the local agent of a British Resistance, should such a movement have become a reality. D'Arcy House became a temporary military base for eight officers and two hundred men of the Cameronians. Weapons and explosives were stored in the grounds and emergency food supplies in the garage.

War or no war, her output was prolific, and she produced twenty-six Campion novels, plus seven others, and a number of novellas, not to mention sixty-four short stories, numerous articles, and a wartime book about England (and especially Tolleshunt D'Arcy). Essex certainly took pride of place in much of her work. All this despite a thyroid condition.

Margery's work heralded an interest in psychological novels such as those produced by such writers as Ruth Rendell, P.D. James and Minette Walters. Her books show her interest in class, gender, family and politics. Worship of money, masculinity in crisis, strong women – they all feature. It was Margery who could be said to have invented the serial killer novel in *The Tiger in The Smoke* (1952), and this book attracted the most critical acclaim. Although grouped among the Golden Age of crime writers, her language was particularly earthy, and Christopher Fowler (in *The Book of Forgotten Authors*) recommended keeping a copy of Brewer's *Phrase and Fable* close by! What he describes as "The Plum Pudding Principle" sums up her success, a principle of introducing a plum every few pages to avoid too much stodge.

Away from work, she had to contend with domestic problems as well as health issues - Pip's infidelities, clashes with the Inland Revenue, and even perhaps their childless marriage. Not long after writing *The Beckoning Lady*, with its autobiographical elements (1955) illness got the better of her. Finally, she succumbed to breast cancer, and died in Severalls Hospital in Colchester.

Margery was buried in the 14th-century St. Nicholas church in her beloved Tolleshunt D'Arcy.

Another novel was published posthumously (finished by Pip) in 1968 – *Cargo of Eagles*. Some of her work was adapted soon after for cassettes and for radio and in 1989/1990 a successful TV series based on her Campion novels appeared, attracting new, if belated, readers. Peter Davison took the leading role as Campion, with Brian Glover as his ex-burglar manservant, the wonderfully named Magersfontein Lugg (DVDs available!).

Hervey William Gurney Benham (1910-1987) wrote more than a dozen books about Essex, especially about Colchester, e.g. *Essex Water Mills*, and about sailing, his second love, e.g. *The Last Stronghold of Sail*. As the founding proprietor of Essex County Newspapers, he was in the privileged position of owning a company that could print and produce many of his books. As the Colchester-based Editor of *the Essex County Standard* from 1943 to 1965 he introduced a revolutionary printing process: web-offset lithography; as a sailor he was involved in the preservation of Thames sailing barges; and as an amateur bassoonist he encouraged young talent. (merseamuseum.org.uk)

SABINE BARING-GOULD 1834-1924

While the name Baring-Gould may not be too familiar, he has to be included because of his prolific literary output (with many of his books still available on Amazon 100 years after his death) and the still-remembered decade he spent in Essex. However, Baring-Gould was born into the landed gentry in Devon, and educated at home as well as at schools in Germany and France when his family were travelling. He gained his M.A. at Cambridge in 1860, followed by holy orders in 1864 and a curacy in Yorkshire, learning six languages including Icelandic along the way. He married the young working-class Grace in 1868, perhaps an unlikely choice, first sending her off to be educated, though whether this contributed to the success of their marriage, which produced 15 children, is debatable.

His move to the rather remote St. Edmund's in East Mersea in 1871 could be considered a form of exile, because his radical views had upset some of the Anglican church's hierarchy. He had in fact already upset his father by not choosing to inherit the role of squire in Devon. By the time he moved to Essex, he had already written at least three novels, plus *The Book of Werewolves*, the latter one of his many interests which included ghost stories, local history, archaeology, folk stories, folk songs, legends, myths, and vampire stories – his 1891 story about *Margery of Quether* was England's first vampire story, six years before *Dracula*.

Certainly, during his ten years at East Mersea, he became a well known figure in the area. The author, Lucy Lethbridge, wrote about Baring-Gould in *The Oldie* in July 2018, describing him as "hawk-nosed, in buckled shoes and velvet breeches" with a number of other sources referencing him more literally, i.e. as hagiographer, antiquarian, novelist and eclectic scholar. It seemed he often complained about the cold environment, and was convinced that living on the marshes had a detrimental effect on the mental capacity of the local population, with the local inhabitants being "dull, reserved, shy and suspicious." To add to his uncomplimentary opinion, his autobiography refers to his time in East Mersea as "Ten Years On The Mud." In the Sabine Baring-Gould Appreciation Society Newsletter 1991-1992, his niece Irene Widdicombe* describes him as an eccentric, with "a bell-like singing voice."

Baring-Gould was said to write while standing at his lectern, and this may have been an inspirational choice when writing the many hymns for which he was responsible, including "Onward Christian Soldiers" and "Now The Day is Over," the latter apparently written to be played on the bells of St Edmund's Church. While his years in Essex may not have been his favourite, the landscape inspired the most popular, and enduring, of his novels, *Mehalah* in which he wrote rather romantically of the area as having a "purple glow" stealing "over the waste … every creek and pool royally fringed with sea aster." John Betjeman and John Fowles have both reviewed it favourably, and Fowles mentions the kind of reference that illustrates Baring-Gould's style of social commentary, i.e. that the two Church of England clergymen in it are "treated with a contempt bordering on disgust" (quoted in a thesis by Troy Nelson White on file at the University of Warwick.) The novel is a Victorian Gothic classic, seemingly based on a real young woman who lived on a barge with her parents. It is set on Ray Island, close to Mersea Island, during the Napoleonic wars, and has been compared by some to *Wuthering Heights*. This was certainly written during his years in Essex and was published in 1880, but was among some 80 works published during that decade, including books of sermons, volumes of folk songs, and hundreds of short stories.

When his father died in 1881, Baring-Gould returned to Devon and became both squire and parson of the village of Lewtrenchard, following in his father's footsteps. (The family estate is now a hotel). From hereon he produced well over a hundred more novels, biographies and non-fiction works including histories of Devon and Cornwall, and the impressive multi-volume *The Lives of the Saints.*

Baring-Gould died in 1924, a few days before his 90th birthday, and is remembered in Devon primarily for his archaeological studies as a founder member of the Dartmoor Exploration Committee. As for Essex, in 1970, The National Trust bought Ray Island and it is now a nature reserve, but its association with *Mehalah* will continue while the book (among others) is constantly re-printed.

*Comedian Josh Widdicombe is a descendant.

NINA BAWDEN 1925 – 2012

Nina was born and brought up in Goodmayes, Ilford, in a house she described in *Essex Life* magazine in September 2009 as "perfectly comfortable, but unexciting ... I really felt I belonged in a fine, ancient house, if not a castle." Her mother, a teacher, also found the area and neighbours suburban because there were no books in the houses. Although she liked to play in a nearby farmer's field and enjoyed day trips to Southend or bus rides to the cinema in Romford with her grandmother, she was interested in writing from an early age, writing plays for her toy theatre, and one for her primary school. Nina was also interested in art, and drew pictures based on the stories she read, some of which were exhibited at the Royal Drawing Society. Her first words in print were a letter for the *Ilford Recorder* at the age of 14, which gave her great encouragement.

She passed her eleven plus, a huge relief to her mother, who, according to the *Guardian* in 2012, saw education as a way out of falling into poverty. This meant she attended Ilford County High School, but at the outbreak of war just a few years later, her school was evacuated, initially to Suffolk and then to Wales. Nina experienced several different billets, and enjoyed her years as an evacuee, delighting at the warmth of the Welsh and learning a lot about the poverty in the Welsh communities. She used her experiences years later in her most popular children's book *Carrie's War* (1973) which won the Phoenix Award. She returned home in 1943 and resumed her studies, this time at Oxford, focusing initially on French, then moving on to philosophy and politics. While there, she shared fire-watching duties with a fellow student, Margaret Roberts (latterly Margaret Thatcher).

Nina married Henry Bawden, an ex-serviceman, in 1946, a few months after graduating and the marriage produced two sons, Nicholas and Robert. It was while they were babies that she started to write seriously, focusing initially on short stories, utilising the boys' sleeping time. Her first (adult) novel was published in 1953, *Who Calls The Tune*, receiving an advance of £75, not bad for the time. However, just a year later the marriage ended in divorce. She re-married in 1954 – a journalist, Austen Kark, travelling with him widely. (He became Head of the BBC World Service). They had a home in Greece, but settled first in Weybridge, where she was a magistrate, then Islington, with no apparent thoughts of returning to Essex. This was a happier marriage, the couple having much in common, and producing a daughter named Perdita.

In the years with Henry, Nina wrote a further 22 adult novels and 20 children's books and she was not only shortlisted for the Booker Prize (1987) and the Lost Man Booker (2010) but she also served as a Booker judge. Both of her shortlisted books, i.e. *The Birds in the Trees* and *Circles of Deceit*, feature a schizophrenic character, utilising her experiences with her son Nicholas, who committed suicide in his mid-thirties. Also utilising her own knowledge, she wrote *The Peppermint Pig* (1975) which features her mother's Norfolk childhood, winning the *Guardian* prize for children's fiction. Similarly, *Afternoon of a Good Woman* (1976) made good use of her magisterial experience. In 1989, she wrote *The Outside Child*, based on her discovery when she was 25 of a half-sister from her father's first marriage.

Nina was elected a Fellow of the Royal Society of Literature in 1970, and made a CBE in 1995. In 2004, she was awarded the Golden PEN Award for a lifetime's distinguished service to literature. *Carrie's War*, *Circles of Deceit* and *Family Money* have all been televised, and *Carrie's War* was a film in 2003.

Less happily, she and her husband were involved in the Potter's Bar rail crash in 2002, which killed seven, including her husband, and injured 76, including Nina. She recovered well from her injuries, though they left her with limited capacity for long hours spent typing, and she campaigned long and hard for justice for the affected passengers, with a final admission of liability from the train company two years later. She even wrote a book about the experience in the form of a letter to her husband *Dear Austen*, in 2006. More sadness followed when her daughter, Perdita, died of cancer just months before Nina herself finally succumbed to ill health and old age.

As a child in Ilford, Nina Bawden wrote her first stories about hunters and princesses rather than the boring bankers and shopkeepers around her, but went on to write about the everyday flaws in adults and children, rather than concentrating on the sentimental. She will be remembered for her down to earth, no-nonsense novels which described life as it is, warts and all.

ARNOLD BENNETT 1867-1931

A prolific writer, Arnold Bennett may have been born and brought up in Stoke-on-Trent – in a bookish, artistic family with eight siblings – but he has a claim to Essex fame because of the years he spent in Essex in the early 20th century. Until then, he worked for his father (a solicitor) from the age of sixteen, moving to similar work in London in 1889 but writing popular serial fiction in his spare time. In 1893 he gave up legal work and began working as assistant editor for *Woman* magazine, being duly promoted to editor-in-chief three years later. His successful career as a novelist began with the publication of *A Man From the North in 1898* and he duly gave up the day job and also moved house – to Bedfordshire.

From there, after spending some ten years in Paris, and marrying a French actress in 1907, he began dividing his time between France and England and ended up buying an imposing red brick Queen Anne house in the village of Thorpe-le-Soken in 1913, a few miles from the seaside resorts of Frinton-on-Sea and Walton-on-the-Naze. This was apparently very expensively furnished, an expense he could afford given the success of his novels up to this point, which included *Anna of the Five Towns*, *The Old Wives' Tale* and the first two of his *Clayhanger* novels (all these set in the Potteries like much of his work). He wrote to an American friend that "the English ... will wonder why the madman had three bathrooms in a house so small" but the reason was a visit he had made to the U.S. In the same letter he declared that he was going to install himself there for "everlasting" and that his death would cause a "sensation in the village" ... but the sensation, such as it was, was of a different kind, because Bennett and his wife parted in 1920, prompting him to sell up and move on.

While in Thorpe-le-Soken, however, he also bought a yacht, *Velsa,* and, in its log, described the River Blackwater: 'it is a noble stream, a true arm of the sea; its moods are more various, its banks wilder, and its atmospheric effects much grander. The season for cruising on the Blackwater is September, when all the village regattas take place, and the sunrises over leagues of marsh are made wonderful by strange mists.' Bennett also kept a journal, and in September 2013 he wrote about a visit to the popular and select Frinton golf club, describing it as having "miserable architecture ... no accommodation for chauffeurs ... too small ... [with a] common tea room, devilish cold in winter." He was more complimentary about the course which he described as "beautiful [with an] immense sense of space [and] sense of a vast organisation [spoiled by] a rotten little three-cornered flag flying F G C instead of a superb standard ... [although] the women in white or gay colours were not unattractive."

During these war years, he was spending time in the Ministry of Information in London as part of the war effort, and was put in charge of propaganda in France. Although he devoted considerable energy to the work, his misgivings about the war become apparent in his 1918 novel: *The Pretty Lady*. Similarly, his misgivings about accepting a knighthood for his war-work surface in one of his plays, *The Title,* a success in London in 1918, which refers to all "honourees" as "rascals, millionaires and chumps."

Bennett also found time to write the third of his successful *Clayhanger* novels, *These Twain*, while in Essex. He was the most financially successful writer of his era, regularly staying at the Savoy in London, and numbering such luminaries as H.G.Wells, George Bernard Shaw and Thomas Hardy among his friends. Regarded as one of the finest of all regional novelists, and as famous as J.K.Rowling in his day, he produced in total 34 novels, 13 plays (less acclaimed than his novels) and seven volumes of short stories as well as contributing articles to some 100 newspapers and periodicals. He even found time to paint, with some of his landscapes of Maldon and Beaumont Quay on display in The Potteries Museum in Stoke-on-Trent.

After separating from his wife, he spent the rest of his days in London, without returning to The Potteries, or to Essex. He found domestic happiness with another actress, and the union produced a daughter in 1929, although he never got round to divorcing his wife. Bennett died in his flat in Baker Street of typhoid after drinking some dodgy water on a French holiday. A plaque remains in Baker Street, but his ashes were buried in Stoke-on-Trent ... of course.

SAMUEL BENSUSAN 1872-1958

   This author shares common ground, and much of the same era, with Sabine Baring-Gould. However, it seems only he was held in higher esteem for some reason because he appears in the *Oxford Dictionary of National Biography*. Bensusan was born in Dulwich into an orthodox Jewish family and joined a solicitors' practice in the City of London on leaving school, but was concerned at what he felt were the too severe sentences being handed out and so left the profession to enter the world of journalism. An interest in music secured him a position as music and drama critic, working for the *Illustrated London News* and *The Gentlemen's Journal*, with a move to *Jewish World* as editor from 1897.

It was two years after this that he turns up in Essex, renting a 16th century farmhouse called Moynes in Asheldham on the Essex marshes, from where he could pursue his interest in shooting and country pursuits. This location and these interests influenced his future writing although his first published book was *Morocco* in 1904, a highly illustrated volume about his visit there, which by 2015 had reached 27 editions – one of several books he was to write about his travels.

By 1901, he was staying at the Queen's Head in Bradwell, and by 1906 had moved to Brick House, a rural 50 acre farm at Duton Hill near Great Easton, his home for at least sixteen years according to Richard Pusey in *Essex Rich and Strange*. While at this location, he would have socialised with Lady Warwick of Easton Lodge, becoming her literary adviser (and probably ghost writer) for her book on William Morris and her articles and memoirs. He would also have been in touch with her high-profile transient friends, among them H.G. Wells. Bensusan was a man of many talents, in that a ballet that he wrote, *In Japan*, was performed at La Scala in 1902. Among the many articles he wrote, the subject of farming began to feature, and he became agricultural correspondent for the *New Statesman*. An Essex Record Office blog confirms that he owned a 300 year old cottage in Monk Street, near Thaxted, in 1910 which he rented out to Gustav Holst at the time he was working on *The Planets Suite*. So it appears he was earning a reasonable living at this time, with a wife, Marian, to fund from 1909 onwards.

Bensusan was certainly prolific, producing seven volumes of books about famous artists as well as books about famous cultural figures such as Coleridge, Shakespeare, Rossetti and Charles Lamb. Not to mention over 500 stories of local life, country tales, children's books, gardening, travel books, and rural pursuits such as bee-keeping. He also wrote half a dozen plays based on the life and times of the people in Essex, mainly set around the Dengie peninsula with its low-lying marshes, and was interested in the regional dialect which he used effectively in his writing. Apparently, he even managed to write a 25,000 word guide book for the British Empire Exhibition of 1924 in just five days (according to the *ODNB*).

Throughout the 1930s and 1940s, Bensusan produced his volumes of Marshland tales, featuring the fictitious villages of Maychester (probably Bradwell) and Market Waldron (probably

Maldon), with a more controversial book, *Back of Beyond*, in 1945, referring to the "slavery of farm workers". A busy man, he wrote several novels at this time while also serving as the deputy chairman of the Lexden and Winstree bench at Colchester.

Author Stephen Nunn wrote about Bensusan in the *Maldon Standard* in May 2021, referring to his living in the 1940s at Godfreys in the village of Langham near Colchester, with an additional residence in affluent Kensington in London. Godfreys was apparently a property set in 50 acres with a croquet lawn, orchards and hives, plus 20 acres of woodland. During the war, much of this woodland was cut down, the Land Girls arrived, and so did the noise of overhead planes heading for Europe from the nearby Boxted airfield. The Langham area features prominently in Bensusan's diaries and unpublished autobiography which are held at the University of Essex.

Bensusan was still writing articles and plays and books about Essex in the 1950s, but he died in St. Leonard's, Hastings, on the South coast. According to his obituary in *The Hastings and St. Leonard's Observer* in December 1958, he and his wife had "lately taken a house in [Westfield Lane] St. Leonard's" but "then he had to go into a nursing home." The obituary refers to Bensusan's "keen interest" in the local municipal orchestra and his regular attendance at their concerts, and mentions not only that he was "a critic and lover of music" but that he was "one of the early members of the Twenty Club, the literary society formed in 1924" and that he was "known as The Laureate of the Essex Marshes." Not a bad tribute.

John Betjeman compiled a book on the churches of England in 1958 and personally wrote the introduction to the chapter on Essex's churches, based on his own experiences. He wrote fondly not just of the churches but of the county's towns and villages and its architecture. An oft repeated quote of his is that "The Pier is Southend. Southend is the Pier" and this may be one of the reasons that one of the pier trains was named after him in 1986, although no doubt this was also influenced by his joining in the campaign to save British piers in 1979.

URSULA BLOOM 1892 – 1984

Ursula Bloom, long-time resident of Frinton-on-Sea, was in the *Guinness Book of Records* for several years as the world's most prolific female writer, having had some 560 books published, most of them romantic novels. She also produced short stories, plays for radio and stage, and twenty non-fiction books. Her early years however were not spent in Frinton. She was born in Chelmsford, where her father was the curate of Springfield. The family moved to a rectory near Stratford-upon-Avon when Ursula was a toddler, but it appears that her father was a serial womaniser, and her mother left him before the Great War, and moved with Ursula and younger brother Joscelyn to St. Albans, which stretched them financially. A couple of years later, they found a more suitable rented house in a preferable area with a potentially healthier climate: Walton-on-the-Naze.

Ursula was home educated, and published her first book *Tiger* at the age of seven. By the age of eleven she was writing her own children's magazine, distributed among friends. She was also taught the piano and the violin, the former skill meaning that she was helping to support the family finances by playing for a local cinema in Harpenden, near St. Albans, to accompany the silent films.

In November 1916 Bloom married the wealthy Captain Arthur Brownlow Denham-Cookes of the 24th London regiment, a man who could offer her a more comfortable lifestyle. They took a furnished house – called "Poona" - on the seafront at the rather upmarket Frinton-on-Sea with ten bedrooms and servants, and her mother moved to rooms nearby. Sadly, however, her mother died in 1917 not long before Ursula gave birth to her son, Pip, in London, where Arthur had been seconded to the Ministry of Pensions.

The family returned to Frinton at the end of the war, where Ursula had retained a small house in an area full of what she called "pompous, well kept and pleasant" houses. But this was at a time when influenza was killing thousands, and Ursula recollected queues for funerals at the local church. Her nanny, her cook and she herself all caught it, but it was her husband who became alarmingly ill, possibly weakened by his addiction to alcohol. He died in a matter of weeks, and the shock of all these life-changing events meant she succumbed to the helping hand offered by a good friend of her husband's, but the friendship did not go down well with the gossips of Frinton. Ursula was relieved when he returned to his newly-sick wife in Norwich, and the locals were now much kinder to her in her widowed status.

Although she struggled with loneliness initially, she gradually grew to enjoy the single life, dancing the night away in a gang of post-war young things, and, according to her 1970 autobiography *Rosemary for Frinton*, she joined the Frinton "flapper" set in the 1920s. Local hotels were lively with tea dances and ragtime music, and Ursula had been left comfortably off, still able to afford three servants so that she was not tied at home like so many single mothers. Something else she enjoyed at the time was the return of sausages and chocolate to the shops! Nevertheless, she was not entirely selfish as she helped out voluntarily at a convalescent home for wounded war veterans that was opened by a friend of hers in Frinton. (See also her 1940 autobiography *No Lady Meets No Gentleman*.)

By the 1920s, the home had closed, and Ursula found she had famous neighbours (e.g. Gladys Cooper) and the town had famous visitors that she met including Winston Churchill and the Prince of Wales. She was also travelling farther afield when it came to dancing, to dance halls in Colchester and London. However, deciding to knuckle down to something a little less frivolous, and pursue a vague interest in writing, she produced her first novel by 1924 (*The Great Beginning)* which gave her a £25 advance and what she described in her autobiography as "royalties at unbelievable rates" plus an option for another three books. This started her aimed output of at least two books per year, although she sometimes wrote five times that number.

Her second husband was Commander Charles Gower Robinson, RN, who she married in 1925. They were both fans of dancing – and motorbikes, enjoying making the eighteen-mile ride to Colchester in eighteen minutes, or less. Their wedding reception was held at the Beach House Hotel in Frinton.

Apart from her novels, Ursula was now also writing features for nationals such as the *Sunday Pictorial* and *Sunday Dispatch*, and she was variously a crime reporter and an agony aunt as well as the beauty editor for *Woman's Own* regarding herself as a journalist as well as an author. She was very disciplined, aiming for 10,000 words every day, with her husband correcting her spelling! The range of genres she could produce was extraordinary – apart from romances, there were historical novels, hospital novels, biographies and non-fiction on such subjects as needlework, religion, cookery, beauty and careers as well as her own family history. She was also obviously interested in meditation and naturism as, in 1937, she joined George Bernard Shaw in supporting the Gymnosophist Society that promoted nudity.

Frinton during this period was a place growing in popularity with Londoners. Temporary residents included Gladys Cooper and Douglas Fairbanks, and visitors included Winston Churchill, Noel Coward and Ivor Novello. However, naval families had to get used to moving around. The family seem to have spent time in Epping and settled in Harlow at one point in "the coldest house in England," where Pip went to Harlow College. They also lived for a time in Chelsea during the war, more central for her journalistic work.

When they spent time in Malta, where Ursula's husband was stationed for a while, she began to have migraines, and spent some time in hospital. This experience was put to good use in *No Lady in Bed* (1944) which led to several hospital novels under the pseudonyms Sheila Burns and Rachel Harvey. Other pseudonyms included Lozania Prole, Mary Essex, Rachel Harvey, Deborah Mann, and Sara Sloane. While in Malta, Ursula pursued her love of cycling, although apparently it was considered "vulgar for an N.O.'s wife" [Navigating Officer or possibly Naval Officer] to be seen on one - revealed in an article in the *CTC Gazette* in 1959.

Apparently one of her journalistic coups was to discover the whereabouts of Ethel Le Neve (Dr Crippen's mistress) who was living as a housewife in Croydon in the 50s. Her article on the subject was published in the *Daily Mirror* in 1958. Incredibly, Ursula found time to judge contests such as Miss Great Britain as well as needlework competitions (as an accomplished needlewoman who had designed needlework patterns), and advertise products such as Basildon Bond. She also became one of the few authors earning the maximum possible under the Public Lending Right scheme based on borrowings from public libraries.

Her second husband died in 1979, which is when she wrote her last book, *Sweet Spring of April*. Ursula Bloom died at a nursing home in Hampshire, aged 91, leaving a remarkable body of work behind her.

Certainly her life and her books will always be associated with Essex.

ROBERT BUCHANAN 1841-1901

Robert Williams Buchanan's links to Essex begin well after he was an established novelist, poet and playwright but they are well-established. Born in Staffordshire, by the age of ten he was living in Glasgow, and began to write poetry while at boarding school on the Island of Bute, with his first poem published at the age of 16.

His studies at Glasgow University were curtailed by the bankruptcy of his father in 1860, a tailor who became a noted socialist journalist, but Robert had two volumes of poetry published before he was twenty. After his father died, he moved to London to seek his fortune and married Mary Jay when she was a teenager. For the next two decades, and beyond, he was a prolific writer, with a long stream of published poems, reviews, and a total of 27 novels. His second novel, *The Shadow of the Sword,* began its serialisation in the *Gentleman's Magazine* in January 1876 while the Buchanans were living temporarily in Ireland, and was published in November of that year. Its success meant that the family were able to move back to London, and, although his early works had excellent reviews on publication, e.g. *God and The Man*, which dealt with the psychology of hatred (see *The Longman Companion to Victorian Fiction*), they have not really stood the test of time. Incidentally, his last novel (1900), *Andromeda, An Idyll of the Great River*, focuses on Canvey Island in Essex. Buchanan had two collections of short stories published and wrote 53 (!) plays between 1862 and 1906, the most famous being *Sophia*, an adaptation of the novel *Tom Jones*. A full list of his phenomenal output is available on the website, www.robertbuchanan.co.uk.

By 1881, Mary was suffering from cancer and her husband felt that a move to Southend with what he called its "bracing breezes" would help. However, according to J.W.Burrows (in *Southend on Sea and District*), she "bravely refused to have morphia administered" and she died in her husband's arms in November 1882 at their home in Clifftown Parade to "his intense grief". Burrows mentions Buchanan's visits to his wife's grave in Southend, and that he was known to climb the walls when the churchyard gate was locked – and he also mentions his long walks, late nights and endless cigarettes. At this time, Buchanan was commuting between Southend and London because of his work, seemingly intending to make Southend his long-term home, because he rented a country house with eight acres, Hamlet Court, from 1886. This seems to be where *City of Dreams* – an epic poem described by some as a modern *Pilgrim's Progress* - was written. This was mentioned at a Royal Academy banquet upon its publication in 1888.

However, he was also spending time travelling; to France, and to the U.S.A. where several of his plays were performed often featuring his sister-in-law, Harriett Jay (who became an "adopted" daughter during her childhood, although there were also rumours that he actually married Harriett in Switzerland in 1882, reported in the *Paisley and Renfrew Gazette* in April, months before Mary's death!). Harriett did not just star in his plays, she also co-wrote many of them. Financially, he did well from his writing and from his public readings, but did not manage his money successfully and his ventures into theatrical management were unsuccessful. He was declared bankrupt in 1894 - following in his father's footsteps - when living in Clifftown Parade in Southend. His mother lived in a boarding house on the seafront at Southend, but died a few years later, and was buried alongside Mary in St. John's Church, close to where she had been happy in her final years.

Although he moved back to London to be close to theatre-land, he still did some travelling in the final years until settling back in London. In Harriett Jay's biography of Buchanan, she describes his last days, when he was living at her home in Streatham:

"After a ride in Regent's Park, which lasted close upon two hours, we returned home. He partook of a hearty lunch, and then fell asleep in an easy chair beside the fire. He awoke refreshed, and ... proposed that we should cycle again. 'I should like to have a good spin down Regent Street,' he said. Those were the last words he ever spoke, for five minutes later the cruel stroke had descended upon him which rendered him helpless as a little child. For eight months, passed in the endurance of much pain, his life was spared. On the morning of the 10th of June, 1901, he passed away in blessed unconsciousness, in the sixtieth year of his age." (Also see separate chapter re Harriett Jay.)

A report of the funeral was carried in the *Southend Echo* (14th June 1901). His body was taken by train to Southend, with the famous Victorian actor Beerbohm Tree, who had appeared in some of Buchanan's plays, among the many mourners. Shops in Southend were actually closed for the day, showing the level of respect he commanded. He was buried alongside his wife and mother in St John's Church, with a verse from *City of Dreams* as the epitaph on his prominent tomb. The memorial here was unveiled by Harriett in July 1903, and a plaque remains on Byculla House, Clifftown Parade, his last Southend residence.

MARGARET CAVENDISH, DUCHESS OF NEWCASTLE c1623 – 1673

Perhaps remembered more for her eccentricity than her books, Margaret was born Margaret Lucas at St John's Abbey, Colchester, into a prominent family who spent half their year in Colchester and half in central London, with Hyde Park one of their favoured haunts. Her father died when she was two, and her education was at the hands of private tutors, extensive by the 17th century standards in that it included reading and writing as well as singing, dancing, playing music and needlework. The latter skill was responsible for the bizarre velvet dresses she took to designing and wearing.

By the age of twelve, it seems she had written a number of books, none of them published. Her mother had other ideas for Margaret, and she was introduced into court circles, becoming maid of honour to Queen Henrietta, wife of Charles I, travelling with her to exile in Paris in 1644, safely away from the Civil War raging at home. At court, she met William Cavendish, Marquis of Newcastle, a widower some thirty years her senior, the man she married in 1645. Cavendish was the defeated Royalist Commander, a man who had many of his estates confiscated by Parliament, leaving him in financial difficulties. Margaret supported him and they entertained lavishly, and travelled happily together, favouring England and Antwerp.

1648 was a less happy year because her Royalist brother Charles was condemned for treason and executed by firing squad, following the siege of Colchester. An attack on the Lucas family home caused considerable damage. She did return to England in 1651 to try to gain control of her husband's estates but her appeal to Cromwell failed in that her husband was viewed as a traitor to the State.

From hereon, she seemed to focus on her writing and became one of the most prolific female authors and philosophers of the 17th century, at a time of immense political upheaval, unusual for publishing under her own name when most women authors only wrote anonymously. Her first works, *Poems and Fancies* and *Philosophical Fancies,* were published in 1653 showing she was a serious natural philosopher at a time when women were not formally educated in the subject.

The couple settled back in England, (initially in Bolsover Castle in Derbyshire) when Charles II came back to the throne in 1660, and Newcastle's estates were restored. Margaret continued to write poetry, plays, essays and memoirs, none of which she was known to edit. Not everyone was a fan - Samuel Pepys described her poetry as the most ridiculous thing "that ever was wrote" and John Evelyn, another contemporary diarist, described her as a "mighty pretender". Latterly, Virginia Woolf described her as having "futile" philosophies, with "intolerable" plays and "dull" verses, although conceding that "there is something noble and high-spirited as well as crack-brained and bird-witted" in her writing!

Margaret also produced fiction, which was regarded as a tad racy for its time. Works such as *Assaulted and Pursued Chastity*, for example, featured adultery and seduction, with a frontispiece adding to its titillation by promoting her well-developed bosom in a low-cut gown. Her *Blazing World* (1668), set in a science fiction world with its young Empress, is probably her most famous, and successful, work. Her autobiography was published when she was just 33 and there were collections of letters, orations and essays and a large number of plays, not performed during her lifetime, plus a biography of her husband – in fact, her husband also wrote a few plays in later life, which seemed to have been better received.

William Cavendish does not seem to have been deterred by her apparent lack of domesticity, her outfits or her love of philosophical debate, and is known to have found her generous figure particularly entrancing. Margaret was renowned for her outrageous dress sense, her flirtatious manner, and her obscenity-loaded speech, and she was described by Samuel Pepys as "mad, conceited and ridiculous" while also confirming (April 1667) that she was "a very comely woman." Indeed, in time, she became known as Mad Madge... In spite of public ridicule when it came to her work and her appearance, she was the first woman to be invited to attend a meeting at The Royal Society (in May 1667), the National Academy of Science, recognition indeed.

While Margaret may not have spent that many years in Essex, her remarkable output, and her remarkable life, means that she deserves to be included as an Essex author, and indeed the only Essex girl to be buried in Westminster Abbey. (Although she died in Welbeck Abbey, Nottingham, her husband's family seat.)

JOSEPH CONRAD 1857 – 1924

While Conrad may have only spent a couple of years in Essex, these were fruitful years for him and his writing, and such is his fame that he merits inclusion in these pages. Born in what is now Ukraine, his father was also a literary man, having translated Shakespeare into Polish, but Conrad did not follow in his footsteps initially. He joined the French Mercantile Marine in 1874, then the British Merchant Marine, and spent some twenty years at sea.

He started his first novel (*Almayer's Folly*, set in Borneo) while still at sea, his novels often inspired by his travels and by his experiences in the Belgian Congo where he saw the ravages of war, genocide and lawlessness. Conrad seems to have happily abandoned this roving life in 1895, marrying Jessie George, an English typist he had met through family friends in Stanford-le-Hope, in 1896. This was quite a year for Conrad because he lost money following a gold mining speculation, became a British subject, moved to Essex with his new bride, and then found that the small house in Stanford-le-Hope she had prepared for them was what he called "a damned Jerry-built rabbit hutch," not quite the image of a new villa he had been expecting. The area did at least mean he could sail his small sailing boat, *The Nellie*. According to Tom King in the *Southend Echo* (25 September 2008), Essex workmanship and soil conditions between them let the newlyweds down badly. "The doors were badly hung, the walls started to crack, and instead of warming up the resident, the fireplace blew freezing down-drafts of cold air at them." Conrad had obviously not been prepared for what a downturn in his fortunes meant in practical terms. Historians generally agree that this house was in Victoria Road.

Less than six months later, the couple relocated to a more rural and atmospheric timber-framed medieval farmstead in Billet Lane on the outskirts of Stanford-le-Hope, called 'Ivy Walls' complete with orchard, and with established elm and lime trees to keep the wind off the mudflats at bay. This provided Conrad with more space and solitude so that he could complete another four novels, including the well-received *Nigger of the Narcissus*, and begin another two which have become classics: *Lord Jim*, dedicated to his Navy friend from Stanford (G.F.W.Hope), and *Heart of Darkness*, which became the inspiration for the film *Apocalypse Now*.

Conrad had a view of the Thames from his second floor window at a time when it was a dynamic, busy waterway and he used the river and foreshore in *Heart of Darkness* and *Mirror of the Sea*. The former begins with a group of passengers aboard a boat described as a "cruising yawl" – and named *The Nellie!* - floating on the Thames, though the *Heart of Darkness* is Africa, and colonialism. The latter (not published until 1906) is an account of Conrad's sea-going experiences over 20 years and describes the Thames in some detail, e.g. referring to the "barges [which] sit in brown clusters upon the water with an effect of birds floating upon a pond" and suggesting that "romance has lived too long upon this river not to have thrown a mantle of glamour upon its banks." The Chapman Lighthouse off Canvey Island, which was demolished in the 1950s, is also given a mention early on in *Heart of Darkness*, i.e. "The Chapman Lighthouse, a three-legged thing erect on a mud-flat, shone strongly." This particular book has also inspired television features and musical productions.

'Ivy Walls' was the birthplace of Conrad's eldest son Alfred Borys, in 1898, but the family moved to Kent in October that year, to a much smarter inland property owned by a literary friend, Ford Madox Ford. Conrad was now in a much better position financially thanks to the success of his early works. (His younger son was born here in 1906.)

The early twentieth century could be described as a golden age for story-tellers, following in the tradition of Charles Dickens with the continued use of serialisations to help line authors' pockets. In 1919, Conrad sold the motion picture rights to several of his films, which solved any lingering financial problems and enabled him to move into a large Georgian house in Canterbury, where he died in 1924 following a heart attack.

The house in Billet Lane, 'Ivy Walls', was demolished in the 1950s and its site is now a recreation ground, but a plaque was finally erected in 2008 to commemorate this world-renowned and prolific author. There are sixty of his books available to buy on line, including volumes of short stories and essays, but it is Essex in particular that is proud to have a connection with the great man.

William Makepeace Thackeray (author of *Vanity Fair* etc) was not inclined to visit his wife, Isabella, after she developed ante-natal depression in 1840, having given birth to three daughters in quick succession. After years of her being "in care" in France and elsewhere in the U.K., she ended her days in Eden Lodge, Leigh-on- Sea, and died there in 1894 after more than 25 years, outliving her absentee husband by over thirty years. He made good use of his 52 year life span, producing 69 novels, a number of serials, and hundreds of essays and articles for such magazines as *Punch*.

(GEORGE) WARWICK DEEPING 1877-1950

Warwick Deeping was born in Prospect House, Southend-on-Sea, opposite the Royal Hotel at the top of Pier Hill, moving to Royal Terrace just yards away as a boy. He has written fondly about his childhood as being "nearer to nature than many modern children" with an early morning swim in the Thames as part of his daily routine. His recollections include "running wild on the somewhat wild cliffs, and paddling and digging on the beach."

From the age of ten, he was educated in London at the Merchant Taylors School, Clerkenwell, first of all boarding out but, apparently unhappy with the food and overcrowding, commuting to London from the age of sixteen on the new railway. His academic record was such that his fathe - a renowned surgeon - encouraged him to cram for his entrance exams to Trinity College, Cambridge, by moving to live with a tutor, and there he felt he learnt more in seven months than in the previous seven years. It meant he passed his exams and achieved a B.A. and M.A. at Cambridge.

Although he followed in the family tradition by training as a doctor at Middlesex Hospital (his grandfather was also what we would now call a G.P.), it seems his interest in writing took over because he had his first novel published in 1903. This was *Uther and Igraine,* based on an Arthurian legend, and achieved modest, but encouraging, success. He dedicated this book to Maude Phyllis who he married a year later, and the couple based themselves in and around the Hastings area for a time where Deeping practiced as a doctor for one year, but he very soon took up writing full time when his next two historical novels also enjoyed commercial success. However, for financial security, he also started a landscaping business, according to The Elmbridge Hundred website. Nevertheless, he produced one novel each year until his (hand-written!) output was interrupted by the First World War. Deeping joined the Army Medical Corps in 1915, serving at Gallipoli initially as Captain, and then as Major.

After the war, the couple moved to Weybridge in Surrey. However, Deeping's most popular book, *Sorrell and Son* (later televised), was based on Southend, also utilising his war experiences which he described as "horrific". This novel was turned into a silent film in 1927, with a sound version in 1933, and subsequently adapted for 1980s' television. Four other novels (*Caroline Terrace, Dark House, Slade* and

Mr Gurney and Mr Slade) deal with the locality of Southfleet, a probable disguise for Southend. Other novels make good use of his medical expertise, e.g. *Sincerity* (1912).

He wrote more than seventy bestsellers in his lifetime as well as plays and short stories. Many of Deeping's books were published in America and Australia, and a number were translated into several languages, with another four being adapted for the cinema screen. His range covered subjects as diverse as Roman Britain and the Middle Ages. *Sorrell* was in fact his 33rd novel, and his publishers, Cassell, produced an annual spring or autumn 'Deeping' for all his readers. Even John Betjeman appeared to be a fan as he was involved in the (unsuccessful) campaign to save Deeping's birthplace from demolition, saying "I would be prepared to stake my literary reputation on acclaiming the excellence of the early work of Warwick Deeping". In the book *Smugglers Moon*, the author L.E.Jerram-Burrows enthused over *Sorrell and Son* as combining "love, beauty, loyalty, dedication and sincerity" with "poverty, misery, despair, intrigue, sickness and death."

Deeping did return to Southend on at least a couple of occasions in the 1930s and 40s – he opened a 1933 bazaar in support of the new Southend Victoria Hospital and spoke about his father visiting patients in remote villages "by horse and trap" in the middle of the night to carry out emergency surgery in primitive conditions. In 1945 he was back at the hospital presenting prizes to the nurses. These visits were at a time when he was still widely popular, as indicated by his inclusion in the set of Famous British Authors cigarette cards issued in 1937 by WD&HO Wills, alongside such luminaries as J.B. Priestley.

This prolific author died at his Weybridge home, but there is an impressive memorial in St John's Churchyard in Southend, where three siblings were buried. Six further books were published posthumously, promoted by his wife, Maude Phyllis, who outlived him by over twenty years. He left an estate worth over £33,000 and she had a comfortable end to her days with servants and a green Rolls Royce. The Warwick Deeping Appreciation Society was set up in 2000 and was well supported until the death of its founder in 2008. A comprehensive Deeping archive is in Boston University in the United States which includes some original handwritten manuscripts, confirming his international popularity.

DANIEL DEFOE c.1660-1731

Born and educated in London, Defoe is descended from an old Essex family named Foe who had settled in Chadwell, near Tilbury, in the 15th century. Although his father was a prosperous candle maker, it was anticipated that Defoe would enter the nonconformist ministry, given his religious views and religious education, but in fact he followed his father into "trade". He started as a wholesale hosier in 1681, but then, after his marriage in 1684 to Mary (a marriage which came with a generous dowry; and produced eight children), began dabbling unsuccessfully in speculative investments.

As a result, Defoe was declared bankrupt in 1692, and ended up in debtors' prison. He managed to negotiate his way out of prison, and finally set up his own factory in Tilbury in 1694 making roof tiles and bricks on land he had already leased. Some successful years followed, with Defoe able to employ over 100 people, meaning he was able to happily settle in a residence near the banks of the Thames with fine views across the water. This was also a period when his writings became popular, and he was diverse in his works – satirical poetry, politics, the social divide, philosophical essays, and religion, the latter sometimes anonymous as it was often, crucially, in favour of those who chose to worship outside the established Church of England, i.e. the dissenters.

His 1702 publication, *Shortest Way With the Dissenters*, resulted in his arrest (again) for seditious libel and he was fined the equivalent (in today's money) of over £60,000 plus a stint in the pillory, and imprisonment at Newgate. The story goes that his fine was paid, and he was released, after agreeing to becoming a secret agent for the Tories, specifically infiltrating their press! These spells of imprisonment (there was another in 1714) came at a time when his business needed his input, and when he needed a regular income to support his large family, so when he was finally released from prison, his business, his finance, and his reputation, were all damaged.

In between his spells in prison, Defoe's fame as an author grew. He witnessed the Great Storm of 1703 which killed thousands at sea, and wrote *The Storm*, giving witness accounts, regarded as an early example of "modern" journalism. He also contributed to other volumes with either spiritual, social or political elements and started *The Review*, notoriously critical of the Government and the press. (All in all, over 500 titles have been credited to Defoe.)

It was as well he was profiting from his writing, as the tile making business foundered, partly because of his absenteeism but also no doubt partly because the manufacturing practice used meant that the tiles and bricks were being made with Thames silt mixed with ash and cinders, i.e. a porous, and potentially useless, mix.

Defoe's first novel was *Robinson Crusoe* in 1719, prompting a sequel, several reprints, and a serialisation. This was followed by several travel-related novels, and, in 1722, by *Moll Flanders*, potentially the first 'major' novel in English, and set in its early pages in Colchester, an Essex area known to Defoe. This was swiftly followed by his *Journal of the Plague Year*, although this relied on the journals of an uncle as he was too young to be able to recall the amount of detail included.

He is said to have caught a nasty fever on Dengie Marshes while travelling, and seemed very interested in accounts from farmers in such areas as Canvey Island and Wakering suggesting that only long term residents could cope with the surroundings. Even if the men married wholesome ladies used to the fresh air, the women developed the ague within "a year at most" meaning the men had to find another wife, and then another, with one "about 35 years old [who] had already had about fourteen" – wives, that is...

1722 was a good year for Defoe. With the profit from his books, he bought a 99 year lease on hundreds of acres of land at Mile End (now Myland, north of the city centre) from the city of Colchester, along with the timber rights, worth many thousands of pounds. There were several farms on the land and Defoe now diversified into breeding cattle, growing corn and making cheese, butter and honey. He also began selling oysters and producing a range of cloth, showing an interest in trying again with a tile factory in the area although this does not appear to have come to fruition. A few years later, he produced his heavyweight *A Tour Thru' the Whole Island of Great Britain,* which included, for those interested in Essex, a *Tour of the Eastern Counties of England*, with its many first-hand descriptions of rural Essex. Defoe wrote of exploring the Thames estuary and of "men of war ... moored and laid up" on the Thames, but he also explored the Chelmer and Blackwater Rivers, visiting Maldon, Osea Island (laden with game) and Colchester with the "nicest, tho' not the largest" oysters in England. He travelled by boat and on horseback, describing every town he passed through in detail, e.g. Harwich is depicted as a "town of hurry and business" giving a good insight into the county in the early 18th century.

However, by 1728, he was in financial trouble again as a result of his poor management skills. He handed over the Colchester property to one son, and his London home (in Stoke Newington) to one daughter as dowry, but was still being pursued for debts and ended up in uninspiring lodgings in the City of London, where he died following a presumed stroke in 1731, his wife following him to the grave a year later.

Of course his most famous novels have been immortalised on screen in the 20th century, and he is appreciated by both the academics and the populist reader. Several of his novels have never been out of print – for 300 years – which is a huge achievement. Essex was proud to have him.

Rudyard Kipling has a plaque honouring his visit to Goldings Farm at Loughton, along with Stanley Baldwin, in 1877. Although this visit was just a long holiday at the farm, his sister wrote about it as a formative period of his life. Kipling was twelve at the time, and Baldwin, a future Prime Minister of course, was just ten, so these were schoolboys free to enjoy the peace and quiet of the countryside for several summer months, and to befriend local farm boys and gypsies. According to author William Addison, he was sent there to escape the beatings he was receiving at the boarding school he had been attending in Southsea. It is unlikely to have inspired him to write *Jungle Book*, but he did write another 40 novels as well as numerous short stories, and 19th century Loughton and Theydon Bois turn up in one of the latter, *Bread upon the Waters*.

HENRY DE VERE STACPOOLE 1863-1951

This should be a memorable name, but he has slipped from the obvious stream of well-known authors and is now only really known for one particular book, *The Blue Lagoon*, dating from 1908, mainly because there were three film versions (starting with a silent version, and ending with the blockbuster 1998 version with Brooke Shields) and two sequels.

He was born and brought up in Ireland, his Reverend father dying when Stacpoole was just seven, thus becoming reliant upon his mother, along with his seven siblings. One of his brothers and one of his sisters also became writers – William, who wrote children's books, and Florence, who wrote mainly about health and medicine, but these do not have an Essex connection. Initially, he studied literature, but then trained in medicine in London and became a ship's doctor.

According to the *Dictionary of Irish Biography*, Stacpoole simultaneously pursued a literary career, and had five novels published during the 1890s, though none of these were commercially successful. Things changed in 1905 with a popular comic-romance, *Fanny Lambert*, and his 1907 sea adventure, *Crimson Azaleas,* increased his popularity.

After a stint as a G.P. in Somerset, he met and married Essex girl Margaret, also a writer, and they honeymooned in 1907 at the house of a friend in Stebbing Park, near Great Dunmow, in the then rural countryside. While there, they fell for the charms of the 17th century Rose Cottage, next door to St. Mary's Church in Stebbing, and this is where the literary couple settled having also lived for a while in Castle Hedingham in North Essex.

From hereon Stacpoole started to attract literary attention with some success for his next two novels, and then came the publication of *The Blue Lagoon*, which has, incidentally, been reprinted twenty times since. The success meant that he was able to write full time – although he also served as a Justice of the Peace – and became a prolific author.

Apart from novels, he produced translations, short stories, poetry, with some utilising his experience as a ship's doctor, and others recollecting his Irish roots. He also used the pseudonym Tyler de Saix to write *The Man Without a Head*, described as a lurid thriller! (1908).

Altogether, he authored some 60 books, including two autobiographies, and he was a well known name back in the day, with half a dozen other books turned into films. His wife Margaret co-authored at least one of his books: *The Man Who Found Himself*. According to the Summer 2014 edition of *Stebbing Scene*, Stacpoole became a close friend of H.G.Wells who he met while the latter was staying in Essex. Wells is reputed to have visited Stacpoole in Rose Cottage.

Stacpoole and his wife lived in Stebbing until 1922 when they relocated to Bonchurch on the Isle of Wight. Here he was able to indulge his love of nature and botany, and he founded the Penguin Club to study and protect sea birds. After Margaret died in 1934 he presented the village with a pond and bird sanctuary in her memory. Four years later he married her sister, though neither marriage resulted in any children.

He died in 1951 after an operation in hospital at Shanklin, and is buried in St. Boniface Parish Church, Bonchurch. Several of Stacpoole's books are still available on Amazon and elsewhere, and as recently as 2012 another remake of *Blue Lagoon* (*The Awakening*) received mixed reviews from cinema fans. His Essex home has a blue plaque in his honour referencing him as "Author and Surgeon" but he should be remembered proudly and not just in Stebbing.

JOHN FOWLES 1926 – 2005

John Fowles was born and brought up in Fillebrook Avenue, Blenheim Park, in the coastal resort of Leigh on Sea. His father, Robert, had trained as a solicitor but had felt obliged to enter the family tobacco business in London, commuting there every day in his bowler hat and suit. Robert had met his wife, Gladys, ten years younger, at Westcliff-on-Sea tennis club, and she seems to have been happy to settle for life as a traditional housewife.

Fowles was born one year after the couple married in St. Saviour's Church, Westcliff, but his only sibling, Hazel, did not arrive until he was 16.

Alleyn Court School in Southend was Fowles' first school, where the Essex captain (Denys Wilcox) taught him cricket. Apart from sports, he also seemed to enjoy the academic side of his education. But it was at school that he also developed his lifelong interest in nature, which could be said to have surpassed his love of literature. Nature expeditions were organised by his uncle Stanley, a teacher at Alleyn Court, and Fowles enjoyed hunting for caterpillars and lappet-moths on the Thames estuary marshes. He has also written of "the thrill of hunting for caterpillars among the sloe thickets of the Essex sea-walls near where we lived." His first published essay, 'Entomology for a schoolboy', appeared in the Alleyn Court school magazine in 1938. Bedford School came next, a two hour drive away. Fowles seems to have been the perfect public schoolboy, becoming head boy, and featured as an outstanding cricketer. However, he did admit to being homesick – and also to being bullied. During school holidays he joined his family in Devon, where they had been evacuated. After Bedford came military service, then Oxford University, where he studied French and German.

He acquired a reputation during his lifetime for criticising his dull background, its crassness and suburban nature. The very first line of Fowles' journals, written when he was 23, shows the writer's discontent with provincial 50s England: "This so dull life, mingled with hate and annoyance and pity." Although he lived with his parents until the age of twenty-three, his own life thereafter was anything but dull. For the last year of the Second World War he attended Edinburgh University and then did eighteen months' military service in the Royal Marines, another hateful experience. Finishing his education at New College Oxford, his prowess in languages secured him firstly a teaching job at the University of Poitiers in France and then at Anargyrios College on Spetsai. He wrote *Journey to Athens*, a novel (unpublished), while there in 1951-2 but, more importantly, it was also the place where he fell for Elizabeth, the wife of a fellow teacher. Two years later, back in London, Elizabeth left her husband and her two-year-old daughter for Fowles, in spite of his acknowledged affairs with a couple of his students.

They married in 1954 and Fowles taught at St Godric's in London (a secretarial college), writing in his spare time, with the usual rejections. Until, that is, *The Collector*, a mix of thriller and conflict about a butterfly collector, was published in 1963 – the sale of the film rights enabled him to give up the day job. Fame, and affluence, came quickly although of course Fowles was already in his late 30s. Suddenly, he was travelling to Hollywood to see his novel being made into a film with Terence Stamp, and attended London parties with celebrities. Unsurprisingly, he promptly resigned his teaching post and became a full-time writer.

The success of this first novel enabled Fowles to sell the film rights to his next, *The Magus,* before it was even finished. He had published a non fiction volume in between featuring psychological studies. The book, published in 1965, was based in part on his experiences in Greece, but was apparently inspired by Shakespeare's *The Tempest* and further illustrates Fowles' interest in psychology. But, ironically, this film (starring Michael Caine) was less successful than the first. However, in the 1960s, John Fowles remarkably reached the bestseller lists on both sides of the Atlantic.

By 1968, the couple were living in Dorset, although Elizabeth didn't like the county that much, especially in the winter, and Fowles really wanted to live in France. Instead, they settled, after a couple of moves, for a palatial Georgian mansion in Lyme Regis close to the cliffs of the Jurassic coast, with an enormous garden. As Fowles' muse, critic and editor, Elizabeth had an influence on his next success, published in 1969: *The French Lieutenant's Woman*. The option money for the film rights for this, and an advance for another novel, *Daniel Martin,* earned him a remarkable half a million dollars in one week in 1977. Fowles may not have written many novels (four between 1970 and 1990) but it seems he didn't need to, although he did a lot of writing in other genres, e.g. essays, translations and reviews. He was also kept very busy by the position he took up in 1977 as curator of the local museum at Lyme Regis and by his ardent campaigning for conservation in all its forms.

Elizabeth died of cancer in 1990 shortly after diagnosis, and Fowles, after a year of grieving, got involved with several much younger women. Eventually, however, in 1998, he married a family friend, Sarah Smith. He had his own health problems, including a stroke and heart surgery, and had become reclusive, but Sarah encouraged a return to his writing. Inevitably, he did not repeat his successes of the 1960s and 70s, although there were two lesser novels in the 80s, and a collection of essays (*Wormholes*) and his *Journals,* in two volumes. Fowles died of heart failure at Axminster Hospital, Devon, on 5 November 2005.

Although he had no children of his own, Fowles had stayed in touch with his step-daughter, in spite of the unpromising start to their relationship. On the subject of family, it is interesting that his father had also written a novel, based on his Great War experiences, which was never published. Despite Fowles' scornful attitude towards his parents and his upbringing - and towards Leigh-on-Sea - he used fragments of Robert Fowles' battlefield descriptions in a passage of *The Magus*. A belated compliment? It would seem so. And his home in Essex has a plaque to ensure he will not be forgotten in the county of his birth.

Tony Holland (1940-2007) achieved fame as the creator of *EastEnders* (with co-writer Julia Smith) and, having lived in Dalston, East London, had the right background to have been chosen. However, he was born in Shoeburyness, near Southend-on-Sea, one of three sons of an army instructor and the family moved around with his father's job. According to *The Guardian* (3rd December 2007) Holland went to twenty schools as a result, one of them in Romford. Predictably, he started life in the Royal Army Medical Corps, but turned to acting for a while before deciding that his future lie in script-writing and he worked on *Z Cars*, *Angels* and *The District Nurse* (with Smith) before being offered to start up *EastEnders*. Note that at the start of *EastEnders*, Holland was living in Walford Road, Dalston, hence the location's name [diamondgeezer.blogspot.com]. Holland created more than half the soap's characters of the 1980s, many based on people he knew. (*The Herald* 6th December 2007). In spite of the later short-lived series *Eldorado*, he was awarded a Special Achievement Award at the British Soap Awards in 2002.

MARGARET GATTY 1809 – 1873

As the daughter of the rector of Burnham-on-Crouch and nearby Southminster, Margaret spent the first ten years of her life in Essex. Her father, Alexander Scott, had been chaplain to Lord Nelson on 'HMS Victory' and was said to have been with Nelson when he died. Margaret's mother died when she was two and she was almost entirely self-educated, but to a high level, becoming reasonably fluent in German, Italian, Latin and French. She also had painting lessons and learned how to play the piano, deemed a part of well-bred female education at the time of course.

It was after the family moved to a larger parish in Catterick, Yorkshire, in 1819 that she started visiting the British Museum when staying with relatives in North London. Her span of interests grew even further and she was fond of copying prints, and learned how to etch onto copper. She and her elder sister seemed to have lived quite a social life, as well as helping their father with his curacy duties. It was eventually 1839 when Margaret met and married Alfred Gatty, a young priest. Alfred was expecting to take over the curacy at Southminster, but instead was appointed vicar of the parish of Ecclesfield in Sheffield (i.e. a promotion) and remained there for 64 years! During this time, Margaret bore him ten children, in spite of what would have been seen as her "advanced" age, eight surviving into adulthood.

It is a long way from Essex, then, that Margaret started writing books for children, and when she developed a lifelong interest in seaweed and sundials - obviously a woman of eclectic taste and eclectic gifts. Some of her seaweed collection is at the Natural History Museum in Kensington, London, with one species named after her, and she also wrote books on the subject which she illustrated profusely.

Her first book appeared in 1851, *The Fairy Godmothers*, and she had written a dozen children's books by the time her first seaweed book – *History of Seaweeds* - appeared twelve years later. As a result of her success in writing for children, she edited *Aunt Judy's Magazine*, a new venture, from 1866. By 1868, the profits from this magazine had raised enough to pay for 'Aunt Judy's Cot' at Great Ormond Street hospital. Her *Parables from Nature*, which started life in 1857, became a popular series which continued until 1871.

In 1872, *The Book of Sundials* was the culmination of a lifetime's interest and collecting and which went on to be re-printed and enlarged over several decades. This was a year before her death, believed to be (with hindsight) the result of multiple sclerosis (pmnhs.co.uk). The memorial in Eccleslesfield Church was funded by contributions from children "as a token of love and gratitude for the many books she wrote for them."

As a writer, Margaret Gatty was not a one-trick pony, and Essex can perhaps boast that those first ten years surrounded by the seaweeds in the River Crouch and the sundials of Essex prompted her future fame, if not fortune.

ELINOR GLYN 1864 – 1943

Born in Jersey, Elinor's father died when she was a few months old and her mother returned to her Canadian roots with her two daughters until she re-married and moved back to Jersey when Elinor was about ten. Mostly self-taught, she showed an early talent for drawing and writing, and kept a detailed diary. It seemed she was hoping to mix in higher-status, romantic circles with a husband who shared her interest in mythology and mysticism, but in 1892 she married a man more interested in food, drink and gambling. This was handsome Essex landowner and barrister Clayton Glyn. Around the time of their honeymoon, Clayton apparently "hired the Brighton swimming baths so he could watch the superb naked form of his wife as she swam up and down like a mermaid with her hip length red hair streaming behind her in the water" (according to historian Tessa Aarlen in a web post in June 2014).

Glyn's historic family home was a medieval mansion called Durrington House, part of the Sheering Hall Estate, near Harlow, in Essex, and this was where the couple settled and where Elinor bore their two daughters. Clayton Glyn, despite inheriting debts from his father, enjoyed entertaining and living rather extravagantly, and the couple mixed in the kind of circles that appealed to Elinor. According to *Elinor Glyn, A Biography* (by her grandson Anthony) he enjoyed being Lord of the Manor and she liked to take walks on the estate away from the locals "who had to make obeisance to her". However, she disliked not being allowed to walk through her own woods because of the need to avoid "disturbing the young pheasants"! They lived just fifteen miles from Little Easton, inhabited by Lady Brooke, the Countess of Warwick, who actually recognised the beauty of this red-haired neighbour, and befriended her. Lady Brooke, or "Darling Daisy" as she was known, was one of Edward VII's many mistresses, and a member of an exclusive royal circle which Elinor could now join.

However, this did not help Glyn's debts which continued to grow, but he was saved from bankruptcy by his wife's success as an authoress. Nevertheless, in 1896, living at Durrington House became too much of a financial strain, and they moved to Sheering Hall until 1903 when they moved again to a cottage on the estate called Lamberts.

In 1898, during her second pregnancy, Elinor wrote a series of fashion and beauty articles for *Scottish Life*. But after the birth, Elinor developed post-natal depression, followed by rheumatic fever, and had a pavilion built in the extensive gardens so she could pass her time, while incapacitated, by putting her earlier diaries together into a book: *The Visits of Elizabeth* (1900). The book, serialised in *The World*, was a great success, and Elinor followed it up with four more romantic novels, all of which emphasised the high value she placed on aristocracy.

Her deteriorating marriage to Glyn led her to seek extra marital affairs. Cecil Beaton, writing in *The Times* in October 1974, claims that Clayton started to borrow money from her lovers, which was apparently the last straw for Elinor. She began a relationship with the younger Lord Alistair Innes Ker, who was apparently the inspiration for her most successful, and, at the time, notorious, novel: *Three Weeks* (1907). The writhing on tiger skins seemed to strike a particular chord, prompting the rhyme:

> *Would you like to sin with Elinor Glyn on a tiger skin?*
> *Or would you rather err with her on a different fur?"*

Three Weeks and its raunchy sensuality sold in its millions, despite negative reviews, and Elinor herself appeared in a stage version. It was when she was on stage that she met Lord Curzon who, although apparently besotted with her, led her to think that this could be her second husband after Clayton died in 1915 – until she read of Curzon's engagement to a rich widow from Argentina. She continued to write at least one novel every year to support herself and fund her lifestyle, and established herself as a literary force to be reckoned with by the First World War, with a couple of novels turned into silent films, albeit they were often described as potboilers.

In the meantime, in October 1907, Elinor boarded the *Lusitania* and set sail for New York on her first American tour in order to promote *Three Weeks.* As a well-known, glamorous and sophisticated figure, she began receiving offers from Hollywood. According to Beaton, she possessed "a great gift for making money, but she knew too how to spend it" so she was attracted by the money that the new cinema industry was producing and moved to Hollywood in 1920, severing her ties with Essex. She worked as an extra for a while, but then signed a contract to write a number of screenplays, popularising the term "It Girl" – and, of course, she was involved in directing the filming of her own novel, *Three Weeks*, in 1924.

Elinor did return to the U.K. in 1929 partly because of money owed in U.S. taxes, but also because of her ailing mother, seemingly poised "to make a fresh assault on the British film industry" as it entered the sound era (according to Annette Kuhn, part of the Women Film Pioneers Project). She incorporated Elinor Glyn Productions in 1930 and brought a cinematographer over from Hollywood to produce two talkies at Elstree, but her inexperience and the "creaky plots" meant that she ended up with two flops (*Knowing Men*, and *The Price of Things*, both 1930). At this time she seems to have been living in London, where she continued writing novels and film fan articles until she died at the age of 79.

Elinor produced 38 books - including one on how to avoid wrinkles – many of them in Essex, and deserves a place in its literary hierarchy. She was included in the set of Famous British Authors cigarette cards issued in 1937 by WD&HO Wills, quite an accolade.

P.S. Interestingly, several historians mention that Edward VII would not even allow *Three Weeks* to be mentioned in his presence in view of its scandalous nature, while Essex historian Margaret Mills on Phoenix FM in October 2021 refers to him as "never having read a book until he picked up a copy", generating even more publicity!!!

Erskine Childers born in London, brought up in Ireland, spent some time in Bradwell on Sea in 1903. He stayed at the part-Tudor Bradwell Lodge while writing one of the first known spy stories, *Riddle of the Sands*, which became the most famous of all his subsequent novels. Childers was a yachtsman, known to have smuggled arms into Ireland for the Easter uprising in 1916, and, crucially, an M.P. representing Sinn Fein, becoming one of the leaders of the IRA rebellion against the Irish Free State, resulting in his execution in 1921. Leonard Piper, in *The Tragedy of Erskine Childers*, refers to the author writing of exploring the River Roach on a "grey day" when a sense of "infinite desolation lays hold of the senses" confirming his knowledge of the area.

ELEANOR GRAHAM 1896-1984

While Eleanor Graham was not a prolific author, she was described in *Brittania and Eve* (a "lady's" magazine) as "one of the foremost authorities on children's books in England" - 1st April 1953. She never made a living from her writing, but she made a living from books.

Eleanor and her family moved from Scotland to Walthamstow in 1900 (when Walthamstow was in Essex) and her father took over the editorship of *Country Life*, although her parents separated two years later. Her schooling was at Chingford High School, then the North London Collegiate School for Girls, and finally the London School of Medicine when she was thinking about a career in medicine. Leaving education during the First World War, she spent some time in Czechoslovakia, distributing aid, before returning to focus on her interest in poetry and in writing.

Her first book, published in 1925, was *The Night Adventures of Alexis*, described in the *Aberdeen Journal* (3rd December 1925) as "a jolly story book about the adventures of a little boy called Alexis" which all took place "after he went to bed" and "should appeal to fantasy-loving children." *The Sketch* (16th December) put it on their Christmas list of illustrated gift books for young people.

However, although off to a good start, she was not making a living from her writing and therefore accepted a job at the Bumpus Bookshop in Oxford Street in London in 1927 to run a new "children's room". This was a golden age for children's fiction, though not necessarily for its quality, and Eleanor felt children deserved better, and wanted to improve non-fiction books for children. She was also in a good position to encourage children to take an interest in poetry, which was lacking. While at Bumpus, she is said to have advised Arthur Ransome (of *Swallows and Amazons* fame) to add illustrations to his book to help with sales – and he took her advice.

Four years later, she became a children's book editor for William Heinemann and Methuen, and began reviewing children's books in the 1930s for the *Bookman*, and the *Sunday Times*. Her best known book, *The Children who Lived in a Barn, (1938),* was described as "charming fun" and a "comforting roller-coaster for children" by stuckinabook.com.

Lesser known, and less applauded, were *Six in a Family* in 1935, *Change for Sixpence* (1937), *Adventures in Natal* (a boys' adventure in collaboration with G.G.Campbell 1938), and *The Making of a Queen* in 1940 (about Queen Victoria).

Although working for the Board of Trade during the Second World War, she was offered a job in 1940 as editor of a new children's paperback series by Puffin Books, despite the paper shortage then in place. This took her up to retirement, and she took the opportunity to seek out modern classics, starting with *Worzel Gummidge*. The series was a great success, offering children affordable quality. In 1943, Eleanor moved into a flat in Bloomsbury, the centre of literary London, and was responsible for the still-popular *Puffin Book of Verse*, published in 1953, a book which incorporated 'adult' verse which she knew would appeal to children.

Her name appears as editor and compiler of a number of other books for children during the period, and she gained a reputation for elevating children's writing to a respected literary genre. Eleanor started the Story Biography series for Methuen, contributing her own *The Story of Charles Dickens* in 1952, as well as contributing to Lilian Gask's popular *True Dog Stories* the same year. She also had a semi-autobiographical book published in 1947, based on stories told by her Scottish grandmother: *Head O'Mey*.

When she retired from Puffin in 1961, she moved to River Way in Loughton, near the Essex border, a more rural setting where she could continue to write reviews. Her last children's story was in 1960, *The Story of Jesus,* although she also wrote *J.M.Barrie's Peter Pan: the Story of the Play* in 1962, a literary diversion. But she was not forgotten by literary circles because in 1973 she received the Children's Book Circle Eleanor Farjeon award for services to children's literature. Unmarried, she ended her days in what was then a hospice-type establishment in West London, Hereford Lodge, aged 88.

It seems that children everywhere, not just Essex, should be proud and grateful to Eleanor Graham.

JAMES HILTON 1900 – 1954

James Hilton qualifies narrowly on Essex grounds because of the way some parts of East London were moved out of Essex during his lifetime. He was the only son of Elizabeth and John Hilton, originally from Lancashire. They moved, with baby James, when John became head teacher of Chapel End School in Walthamstow, living in the area until 1920, with Walthamstow in Essex until it was fully incorporated as part of Greater London in 1965. It was his father who, in part, inspired Hilton's greatest success story - *Goodbye Mr Chips* – but there is much more to Hilton than this.

Hilton's early education was at an elementary school in Walthamstow and he has written in his autobiography (*To You Mr Chips*) of the "prevalent smell of ink, strong soap, and wet clothes" but, for all that, felt he learned more there than at his subsequent grammar school (Monoux, also in Walthamstow). He also wrote that while at his first school, he "spent an hour a week on botany which was an excuse for wandering through Epping Forest in charge of a master who, in his turn, regarded the hour as an excuse for a pleasant smoke in the open air." He remembers from that time "lovely hours amidst trees and bracken" while from Monoux memories are of a fondness for Latin, and of the building being sandwiched between a pickle factory and a laundry.

In 1914, he won a scholarship to Haileybury College (near Hertford) which had a rifle range and an Officer Training Corps (bearing in mind the year...); as a pacifist, his father objected and so Hilton was allowed to choose his own public school, deciding on The Leys in Cambridge, from 1915, still quite a distance from home. Here he began writing short stories, and he edited the school magazine, moving on in 1918 to Christ's College Cambridge where he read English and History, securing his first published work early on – an essay in the *Manchester Guardian*. While at Cambridge, he was said by his schoolmates to cycle the 35 miles or so to familiar Epping Forest to see his girlfriend, without the knowledge of his housemaster.

His first novel *Catherine Herself* was published in 1920 while he was still at Cambridge. In the same year, his parents moved to Woodford Green (when it was still in Essex!), and he returned to live with them for ten years while pursuing a career as a journalist writing for such newspapers as the *Irish Independent* – and continuing to write novel after novel, without receiving much acclaim.

Once focused on writing fiction full-time he had his first major success: *Lost Horizon*, his ninth novel, inspired by a visit to North Pakistan. This was published in September 1933, featuring a utopian paradise in the Himalayas which he termed Shangri-La, a phrase now in common usage, which is the Tibetan word for snowy or secret mountain pass. This won the prestigious Hawthornden prize, and resulted in a commission from *The British Weekly* for a short story for their Christmas edition. For inspiration, Hilton went for a bicycle ride in Epping Forest on a foggy winter morning until an idea "bobbed up" and, in just four days, he produced the first version of *Goodbye, Mr Chips* which spans some sixty years in the life of a schoolmaster and which became popular in the U.S.A. as well as in the U.K. The 1939 film version won Robert Donat an Academy Award for his role as Chips.

The success of *Lost Horizon* (which had five film versions altogether) and *Goodbye, Mr Chips* in the U.S. prompted Hilton to visit the country, and he found himself a literary agent in New York the same year that he married his first wife, Alice (1935). A year later, he was settled in Hollywood and was adapting *Camille* for Greta Garbo! He became a sought-after scriptwriter in Hollywood. Additionally, his *Lost Horizon* was filmed in 1937 by Frank Capra, now counted as a friend, like romantic lead Ronald Colman, who also starred in the film version of *Random Harvest* in 1942. These may have been sentimental versions of his novels but they secured Hilton financially at a time of the golden age of the movies, and meant that he never returned to the U.K. to live.

One of his most successful screenplays was that for *Mrs Miniver*, starring Greer Garson, another actress he would come to view as a friend. He won an Academy Award for his work on this war story in 1942. His 1941 best-seller, *Random Harvest*, about the First World War, was filmed soon after, again featuring Greer Garson, and winning Ronald Colman an Oscar nomination. This book, incidentally, mentions the trees in Epping Forest, referring to them as a "darkly etched panorama that grew brown and then suddenly green as spring advanced."

Hilton's life had certainly moved on since those days on his bicycle in Woodford Green, although this was where he wrote his two most successful novels, of course: in total he produced 22 novels plus a number of plays. His novels were described in an article about him in *This England* in Autumn, 2000: "rich in memorable portrayals of people and places drawn with affection and insight" and "quiet, reflective stories depicting the lives and loves of ordinary people."

Less successful was his domestic life, because he divorced Alice in 1937 and married a young starlet seven days later, the second marriage lasting just eight years. However, his first wife and he were re-united in his final years, and she was with him when he died of cancer in California in 1954, a year after his last novel *Time and Time Again*. As recently as 2,000 one of his novels was reissued in paperback: *Murder at School*. A plaque marks his Woodford Green home, and the James Hilton Society continues to promote his work.

JOSEPH HOCKING 1860 – 1937

An elusive man, this one, but with 82 books listed on lutheranlibrary.org and nine years spent in Woodford Green (when it was in Essex!), he just has to be included. Largely forgotten now, he was popular in his day.

He was born in Cornwall, the youngest of seven, and started his writing with small books for the local Sunday school, but began his working life as a land surveyor. However, it was his interest in the church that resulted in his studying at the United Methodist Free Churches

College in Manchester, becoming ordained in 1884. From hereon he travelled around England, meeting his wife, Annie, along the way: they married in 1888 and had five children.

Hocking's interest in writing did not dissipate, however, and he started writing novels while working as a preacher. His first was published in 1887 – *Harry Penhale: The Trial of his Faith.* From here he published one or two books every year, not all of them on religious topics. Some were contemporary novels (e.g. *Tommy, A War Story* 1916), some were romances (e.g. *Rosemary Carew: Just A Love Story* 1925), some historical (e.g. *Follow the Gleam : a tale of the time of Oliver Cromwell* (1903), and others were adventure stories (e.g. *Mistress Nancy Molesworth: A Tale of Adventure* (1898). In her *Great Church Crisis* dissertation of 2009, Bethany Tanis points out that Hocking's popularity exceeded that of Thomas Hardy. Interestingly, Silas Hocking, a sibling, was the first writer to sell a million copies of his novel *Her Benny* – in 1879, and three of Hocking's daughters were also writers.

Around 1900, the family settled in Woodford Green when Hocking took on the ministry of Woodford Green Union Church. According to the *Woodford Times* of the 7th March 1902, he first had to commit to a year as a trial run, and if he filled the church for three Sundays each month, the pastorate was his. Fill the church he did! A list of his services was published in the *Woodford Times* and he also earned money as a public lecturer, often promoting Sunday cycling and generally trying to update the church 'rules.' The *Woodford Times* promoted his books regularly, comparing him with Sabine Baring-Gould, with Thomas Hardy, and with Robert Buchanan (all featured elsewhere in this book). The 7th March issue mentioned above describes his novels as "stamped with striking and original individuality. Bold in conception, pure in tone, strenuously high and earnest in purpose, daring in thought, picturesque and lifelike in description, worked out with singular power, and in nervous and vigorous language, it is not to be wondered at that Mr. Hocking's novels are eagerly awaited by a large and ever-increasing public."

While at Woodford, Hocking became a prime mover in having the church rebuilt in 1904 by the arts and crafts architect Charles Harrison Townsend. He remained in Woodford until 1909, until his health prevented him from carrying on, but in fact he went on to recover and continue preaching across the United Kingdom, even travelling to the Middle East in his declining years. He returned to his roots in Cornwall around 1911, and died there in St Ives in 1937. Hocking had continued his prolific output right to the end, with three books published in 1936: *The Squire of Zabuloe, Deep Calleth unto Deep,* and *Davey's Ambition.* One obituary, in the *New York Times,* referred to him as "the author of many novels of a simple, old-fashioned type describing the middleclass life of his day." This certainly seemed to have been his aim, and many of his books are still available online.

The Foyle family – of Charing Cross Road bookshop fame – owned a beach chalet and a holiday home at East Mersea, the latter called 'The Thatch'. Christina Foyle lived at Beeleigh Abbey in Maldon, the 12th century home she had inherited from her father on a 400 acre estate alongside the River Chelmer. Having established the renowned Foyles Literary Lunches, Christina died at home in 1999, aged 88, and left the Abbey to the Foyle Foundation, a charity for learning, education and art, although her nephew, Christopher Foyle, bought it back again at market value. (maldonandburnhamstandard.co.uk)

Note: there is a branch of Foyles in Chelmsford.

SHEILA HOLLAND 1937 – 2000

Born Sheila Coates, this prolific author had a variety of pseudonyms during her writing career, probably the best known being Charlotte Lamb. However, some readers may know her better as Sheila Lancaster or Victoria Wolf or Laura Hardy.

Her roots are in Dagenham, one of those urban areas now pretty much absorbed into Greater London. Sheila's first school was St. Vincent's in Dagenham, followed by the Ursuline Convent for Girls in nearby Ilford. Her father worked at Ford's Dagenham factory but her parents separated when she was young and she was brought up mainly by an aunt and uncle (*Daily Mirror*, 15 September 1995).

In an article in the *Dagenham Post* (20th September 1995) Sheila wrote that she "loved Dagenham" and thought she lived "in a village. There were roads of nice little houses, no tower blocks. No-one had cars in those days and we used to play out in the middle of the street." She was the eldest of eight children and said she relied on memories of her childhood in Valence Avenue in Dagenham "to write about the childhood" of her heroines. However, in the *Daily Mirror* interview, she admitted to having had to share a bed with her three sisters, sometimes surviving on "watery cocoa and bread." During the war years, the children did stay with relatives when deemed necessary.

Her first job was working for the Bank of England, where she was to take advantage of their huge library during her lunch breaks. Her next post was as a researcher for the BBC. When she met and married Richard Holland in 1959, he was a reporter on the *Ilford Pictorial*, and they started married life in a tiny flat near Goodmayes station. They lived on what she called "a cub-reporter's salary" until he moved to *The Times* as sub-editor, enabling them to move to something a little bigger in Clayhall Park, Ilford in 1965. He wasn't the only one who was to earn his living with his writing, however, and Sheila, a voracious reader who was determined to be a writer, sold her first novel to Mills and Boon in 1970, the first of 115 for that particular publisher! She had already had a couple of romances published by Robert Hale, but it was the Mills and Boon contract that changed her life: they commissioned her to write twelve books a year (yes, a year) in 1978, and her Mills and Boon sales reached 100 million over the years. What she introduced in the 1970s was a new climax to her romances – it was no longer enough for the hero just to declare his love for the heroine, the heroine wanted and deserved more than that.

This rise in her income, with her income tax at its highest rate ever of 93%, prompted a move to the Isle of Man that same year. In the meantime, Sheila had given birth to five children, including twins. The family had progressed from a three-bedroom house in Ilford to a 26 room mansion (called Crogga) "with a lake covered in water lilies" employing a gardener and housekeeper. The private library held 50,000 books...

Sheila kept office hours, writing quickly to produce a minimum 2,000 words a day, but able to produce 12,000 words a day at her peak by writing through the night and at the kitchen table with the children around her feet (according to *The Guardian* in their obituary of 23rd October 2000). She could actually manage to write a novel, when pushed, in four days. According to the *Post* interview, she managed to take time off once her grandchildren came along, to spend time with them and her dogs. There is an interesting insight into her methodology in the interview because she "works out the plot and characters before" she starts writing, and she writes a synopsis and "stays with it" although she did occasionally change her mind as the book progressed. She also admits that she chose the Isle of Man to settle because she wanted to live in the "English-speaking world" but it suited her well, and was "a far cry from Ilford."

In the 1990s she moved from Mills and Boon to the Penguin group to give her more flexibility so she could write longer novels. (Mills and Boon had a strict limit of 55,000 words.) Altogether, she completed more than 150 novels, a prolific output. Nearly half of her sales were in the U.S.A., a place she visited on several occasions. She may not have achieved the profile of such luminaries as Danielle Steele or Jilly Cooper, but Sheila outsold them both. She believed she saved countless marriages because women had turned to her books "as a fabulous escape route rather than risking a real-life affair."

As Charlotte Lamb, she had not been afraid to write stories that went beyond the bedroom door, and she was not all about cooing doves. She felt she provided "safe sex between the book covers" (*Daily Mirror*) because although men did not want their wives to "sleep with other guys" they didn't mind them going to bed with her heroes! Her stories were often about heroes losing control, heroines at odds with their sexuality, about obsessions and temptation. Even rape and child abuse were not taboo. Her last novel illustrated this (published posthumously) – *The Boss's Virgin*.

Sheila finally stopped typing on the 8th October 2000 when her death was announced at the age of 62. She left behind a huge authorial legacy and a devoted family, with four of her children believed to be still living at home at the time of her death. Her eldest son, Michael, a record producer, had moved to Ilford at some point.

Interestingly, two of her daughters – Sarah and Jane Holland, born in the 1960s – are also writers. Sarah wrote her first book when she was just 18, becoming one of the youngest romantic novelists in history, and has since written 22 romances as well as being a screenwriter, singer and actress. Jane had written 43 novels at time of writing, using various pseudonyms, like her mother, and, like Sarah, has other skills i.e. as a poet and, a tad surprisingly, as a renowned snooker player.

C. Henry Warren (d. 1966). In 1953, the publishers Robert Hale refer to this author as "living in the beautiful village of Finchingfield" because "nowhere else now has power to hold him" although he was born in Kent and had lived in Hertfordshire and in the Cotswolds. These quotes are on the blurb of his book *The Scythe in the Apple Tree*. There are a few notes written by Warren from a house called 'Timbers' in Finchingfield in Essex Record Office dating from the 1950s, and the Finchingfield Guildhall confirmed his living there at that time, but nothing more definitive. Warren wrote over a dozen books about rural and country life, including Essex (e.g. *Content With What I Have*), but also about the West Country and other parts of the U.K. While it seems certain that he did indeed live in Finchingfield at some period, for how long has been impossible to determine, along with biographical information. (The site is now a lavender farm apparently.) His books, however, do survive and are available on line.

FERGUS HUME 1859 – 1932

Although the author of over 140 novels – more than Agatha Christie! - Hume is not a well known name even in Thundersley, Essex, where he lived for well over thirty years. He was, however, actually born in Powick, Worcestershire, where his father was the steward at the County Pauper and Lunatic Asylum. The family emigrated to New Zealand when he was three, and his education led to a law degree, resulting in a job as a barristers' clerk.

Conversely, Hume's interest at that time (1880s) was in writing plays, but he found it impossible to persuade the managers of Melbourne theatres to accept or even to read them. He therefore attempted a novel, thinking this might lead to interest from theatre managers. This was *The Mystery of a Hansom Cab* (set in Melbourne), one of the earliest detective stories written in English. Hume's novel was rejected by a leading Melbourne publisher so he had it privately printed in 1886 and claims it sold 5,000 copies in three weeks. Unfortunately for him, in financial terms, he sold the British and American rights for £50, and a London publisher re-styled itself as the Hansom Cab Publishing Company and promptly sold 25,000 copies in three days, becoming the best selling Victorian mystery novel! This book actually went on to sell 500,000 during his lifetime, establishing him as a best selling novelist. As he had hung on to the dramatic rights, it did mean that it could be produced as a play in Australia and in London, and achieved long runs, so he did achieve one of his aims. It pre-dated Arthur Conan Doyle, who, incidentally, was said to have been inspired by the story to write *A Study in Scarlet* in 1887.

In 1888, Hume returned to the U.K. and settled for a while in London before moving to Thundersley, living in Church Cottage at the invitation of the local Reverend with the impressive name of Thomas Noon Talfourd Major. He has been described as being at the time a "dapper, dandyish fellow with melting eyes and a magnificent wax-tipped handlebar moustache" (crimereads.com). His second novel was a romance, *Madame Midas*, set in Melbourne, which was reprinted twice, although this, and his subsequent novels, half of them mystery and detective novels, never reached the achievement of *Hansom Cab*, which has been reprinted and re-published throughout the 20th century, and was made into a film in Australia as recently as 2012. In 1889, he had some success with a volume of short stories, seemingly inspired by the Jack the Ripper stories in the contemporary press, and set in England: *The Piccadilly Puzzle*. This attracted a couple of scathing reviews, because of its "titillating" portrayal of decadent behaviour of high society. He also continued to write for the stage, with at least three plays produced, including an adaptation of *Madame Midas*.

The range of Hume's novels is actually quite wide-spread with some science fiction, some fantasy and one *(The Year of Miracle: A Tale of the Year One Thousand Nine Hundred,* 1891) about a pandemic in the U.K.! There were also ghost stories that have been compared with Wilkie Collins, but after the First World War, as the Golden Age of detective fiction began with the likes of Christie and Margery Allingham etc. his books sold less and less. His last was in 1926, *The Caravan Mystery.*

Prior to this, in 1915, Hume had moved from Church Cottage to Rosemary Cottage, also in Thundersley, following the Reverend's death. He now lived with a local friend, chemist John Melville, and his wife, renting a room in their bungalow (according to crimereads.com), no longer with the luxury of six rooms and a housekeeper.

His latter years focused more on giving talks to clubs and debating societies and he seems to have managed these despite ongoing health problems. Hume's obituary in the *Essex Newsman* of 16th July 1932 reported merely that he died while shaving, with others referring to the "cardiac arrest" of a "forgotten author". He left an estate worth just £200 plus some small items such as his pipe, and lies in an unmarked grave alongside the Reverend Maley, who had taken over from Reverend Major.

Jeremy Lloyd O.B.E. (1930-2014) started out writing gags for well known comics, but established himself as a sitcom writer when he teamed up with David Croft – producing *Are You Being Served?* and *'Allo 'Allo* as well as *Grace and Favour*. Lloyd was born in Danbury but not brought up there as he was sent to boarding school and then brought up by his grandmother. His mother was a Tiller girl, according to his obituary in *The Guardian* (23rd December 2014) and apparently not the parental type. Lloyd also wrote a couple of film scripts – a Dracula movie which featured David Niven (*Vampira* 1974), and the bare bones of *What a Whopper*, featuring Adam Faith, and made a few brief appearances on film. As a contrast, he wrote the popular *Captain Beaky* books. Married three times, his briefest marriage was to national treasure Joanna Lumley in 1970 – for six months.

HARRIETT JAY 1853 – 1932

Although Harriett Jay's life and work is inextricably linked to that of her prolific brother-in-law, Robert Buchanan, she was a novelist, playwright – and actress – in her own right, and a true Essex girl. Born to an illiterate mother and chalk-pit labourer in Grays, with six siblings, the childless Buchanans (Robert and his wife Mary) seemed to have taken Harriett, Mary's sister, under their wing and she spent more time with them than at home, though not officially "adopted."

The Buchanans moved around, taking Harriett with them, but Harriett's first novel was set in Ireland where they settled for a while from 1873. This was *The Queen of Connaught,* in 1875, published anonymously. It seems to have been generally well received and was followed just a year later by two more Irish tales. The first theatrical collaboration between Buchanan and Harriett was an adaptation of her first novel for the Olympic Theatre in London in January 1877. Harriett made her debut as an actress in a matinee of this production at Crystal Palace in November 1880. According to the *Illustrated Sporting and Dramatic News* (18th December 1880), she appeared on stage chiefly to "realise some of her own creations" starting in provincial theatre in a range of roles. This was not necessarily a good idea, in that the *Eastern Daily Press* of 27th December 1880 said that she "has made a position as a novelist with a single book. She cannot make herself a stage heroine by a single appearance in a single play … [she] has not yet learnt to be a great dramatic actress."

Her next stage appearance a month later was in Buchanan's play, *The Nine Days' Queen,* playing Lady Jane Grey, and had mixed reviews, some scathing, as in *The Era* which was not alone in claiming that while she "may be, and doubtless is, a very able writer… [this] is no training for the stage. Miss Jay … is a raw amateur."

Continuing with her Irish theme, her next novel, no longer anonymous, was an attack on the Roman Catholic church, a very different approach (*The Priest's Blessing*), and was not a success so she reverted to her more romantic style with her next two, the latter utilising her experience in the theatre: *Through the Stage Door* (1883). This was blasted by *The Spectator* on 15th December as "regrettable … could not be read with pleasure and profit."

She continued to pursue a career on stage, and working with Buchanan on adapting her, and his, novels for the stage. They tried American audiences in 1884, but Buchanan's plays did not go down too well there, and nor did Harriett's acting style, especially when she took on male roles from time to time. Her writing was more successful during this period, with *A Marriage of Convenience*, her next novel, serialised in 1884 in *The Lady's Pictorial: A Newspaper for the Home.* The play *Alone in London* was the first to carry Harriett's name as a co-writer with Buchanan, and this was, finally, a success in the U.S. with a two year run.

As a result, Harriett left the U.S. to bring this play to the English stage. Buchanan soon followed her and was instrumental in its run at the Olympic in London. Although she was becoming involved in theatre management as well as acting, it was her writing that earned her a place at the first Literary Ladies' Dinner held at the Criterion Restaurant in London in May 1889.

While living in London in the early 1890s, Harriett was not doing much writing – or acting – and Buchanan was having a number of theatrical disasters, resulting in both being declared bankrupt, she in 1895, a year after him.

By now, Harriett was using an alias, Charles Marlowe, and fortunately had some success with a comic play staged in 1895 at the Vaudeville in London and the Standard Theatre in New York: *The Strange Adventures of Miss Brown*, subsequently published as a novel. Her collaboration with Buchanan continued with intermittent success, and they travelled as a couple (he was a widower by now) to a number of coastal resorts to get away from London. On the death of both her sister and brother-in-law, she effectively retired, apart from producing her biography of Buchanan. But in fact her biggest success as a playwright was yet to come. This was *When Knights Were Bold*, a farce credited to Charles Marlowe, which was a West End hit (at Wyndham's from 1907-1908) and then appeared in theatres around the world on and off for the next 30 years! It was also turned into a film and earned Harriett comfortable royalties.

By 1925, she had returned to her Essex roots, settling in Ilford, deemed more rural than London, and where she was looked after by a housekeeper and a cook as her sight slowly failed. One of several obituaries was in a Canadian newspaper, *The Lethbridge Herald*, and refers to her having a parrot as a "companion", and to the fact that she was "completely blind" by the time she died at her Ilford home in 1932. She bequeathed the rights to *When Knights Were Bold* to her nephew, William, which must have been well received given that it was such a perennial money-maker.

William was one of several nephews at her funeral at St. John's in Southend, along with a brother, where she was laid to rest alongside Robert Buchanan, his mother and her sister Mary. *The Essex Chronicle* (30th December 1932) mentions the funeral arrangements and makes references to her plays rather than to her novels, perhaps reinforcing a comment on the British Library website regarding one of her early Irish novels (*The Dark Colleen*). It merely states that "Harriett Jay was more of a playwright than novelist" – but this should be taken as a compliment.

SARAH KANE 1971 – 1999

Sarah, born in Brentwood Maternity Home, was brought up in Kelvedon Hatch by parents who were practising Christians, which may explain some of her early evangelical leanings. Her father was a journalist but Sarah's initial interest was in acting and she joined the Basildon youth theatre, deciding, as a result, to study drama seriously and took up a place at the University of Bristol. As her preference moved from acting to directing, she followed up her initial first class honours degree with an M.A. at Birmingham University. In the interim, she wrote several short monologues which she performed at the Edinburgh Fringe in 1991 and 1992. These included *Sick,* a shocking monologue about rape, starting her career in the way it continued: with controversy.

In 1994, she became literary associate at the Bush fringe theatre, and was by then living in Brixton. Kane found success with plays such as *Blasted* and *Cleansed* both at the Royal Court in the 1990s. Their disturbing and violent content (*Blasted* included cannibalism and masturbation, for instance, and *Cleansed* was set in a concentration camp), part of a new writing approach, achieved critical acclaim for its honesty, but the press had a field day.

Sarah was a leading member of the In-Yer-Face theatre movement in London which shook traditional theatre up in the 90s, but she was also a lifetime depressive. Combining the two could not have been easy. She was obviously a woman of strong views, a vegetarian, anti-political correctness, and not distinguishing between male and female lovers.

In 1998, *Crave*, about obsessional love, won near-unanimous critical acclaim, and was hailed by many within the industry as one of the finest plays of the year. It contained dozens of references to suicide, and seemed to show her despair of the society in which we live. Certainly her plays, desperately seeking hope, were a wake-up call for British theatre. To quote from *Crave,* Sarah's work showed her to be "feeling the pain of others".

On several occasions, Sarah became a voluntary patient at London's Royal Maudsley Hospital. It was while recovering from a suicide attempt at King's College Hospital in February 1999 that she hanged herself. Confirming the news of her death, her agent Mel Kenyon told *The Stage* (25th February 1999) that the theatre world had lost "a fiercely courageous playwright ... Sarah was a tremendous talent and a kind and generous soul with an immense capacity and understanding of others... She deeply felt the injustices of this world and wrote with great feeling and passion about the dispossessed." Ian Rickson, artistic director of the Royal Court Theatre, added: "Sarah was a profound human being and a true poet of the theatre."

Her obituary, in the same edition, described her as having "marched into British theatre, forced everyone to confront their prejudices and then left... If ever anyone's plays embodied cathartic release, it was Sarah Kane's."

In 2000 her play about suicidal depression, *4.48 Psychosis*, became her swan song at the Royal Court. It seemed appropriate for this briefly flaring, but unforgettable, talent. This play, described as a "75 minute suicide note" (Michael Billington, *The Guardian* 30 June), was adapted for an opera in 2016 and performed at the Royal Opera House. Good writing just goes on and on.

THE KERNAHANS
JOHN COULSON 1858-1943   MARY JEAN 1857-1941

Jeanie and John (known as Jack) Coulson Kernahan lived at 'Thrums', Preston Road, Westcliff–on-Sea from 1889 until just before the First World War. She published her observations on the area in *Vogue*, describing it as the "quiet Hamlet Court Estate" with "wonderful changing skies" near "Southend-on-Salt-Water" which was accessible for London and child-friendly. The house itself was named after J.M.Barrie's birthplace in Kirriemuir.

He was the third of the eight children of the Revd James Kernahan and his wife Comfort, both from Ireland, and was educated at home in Ilfracombe by his father and at St Albans School, quite a distance away.

Kernahan started writing while studying, with some success, leading to a career of writing essays and articles in prestigious magazines such as *Punch* and *The Spectator*. He also wrote poetry, with his early poems included in Alfred H. Miles's anthology of *Poets and Poetry of the Century in 1898.*

Jeanie was educated at home – in Staffordshire - by her father, a maths teacher, and at University College. Rather than maths, however, Jeanie's success lay elsewhere – as a successful novelist. She married George Thomas Bettany in 1878, a publisher's reader, scientific author and lecturer in botany. On his death in 1891, she was awarded a civil list pension in consideration of "his services to the spread of scientific knowledge and of her own destitute condition" (*Oxford Dictionary of National Biography*) and she married Jack Kernahan a year later, after he had taken on her first husband's job at the publisher Ward Lock! (They had one daughter, Beryl Bettany Kernahan.)

The literary Kernahans wrote some books together, including *Tom, Dot and Talking Mouse and other Bedtime Stories* published in 1916, but their individual works were quite diverse. He focused generally on religious subjects, where she was more of a romantic novelist.

A Dead Man's Diary was his first success, in 1890, appreciated by the likes of Conan Doyle, who had been introduced to Kernahan at a dinner party after praising its merits, prompting a lifelong friendship (*Essex Guardian* 17 August 1901). *A Book of Strange Sins* (1893) followed, described by *The Star* as 'palpitating with life. Terrible in their intensity and vivid vivisection of human mind." The combined sales of *God and The Ant* (1895) and *The Child, the Wise Man and the Devil* (1896), seems to have exceeded 100,000, but interestingly in 1897 he wrote the very different *Captain Shannon*, with its specific references to the dynamite hulks concealed off Canvey Island. The book features a cross-dressing Irish anarchist, probably modelled on Oscar Wilde. (Interestingly, Kernahan was the copy-editor of Oscar Wilde's *The Picture of Dorian Gray*, 1891.) Further diversification followed when his *Wise Men and a Fool* was published in 1901, a collection of essays about literary figures such as the Brontes, reviewed in the *Essex Review* as "agreeable reading ... ideal as a gift book."

From 1906, Kernahan campaigned for compulsory military service although he himself had reached retirement age by the time of the outbreak of war. He held down a desk job (recruiting) and returned to writing religious books, with the occasional digression into such as his *Bow-Wow Book of Dog Love* (1912). All of these would have been written while at Westcliff.

As for Jeanie, her first novel was *The House of Rimmon* (1885), about Staffordshire's 'Black Country' followed by more than thirty others, at least one of which, *Trewinnot of Guy's* (1898), a medical story, resulted in a host of what we would now call five star reviews. These included the *Speaker* which refers to her "racy humour" and "vigorous eloquence", and the *Daily News* which called it "well written and well constructed." Much of her work was serialised and she also had essays and poems published in magazines such as *The Argosy*, some of which featured her interest in clairvoyance. She converted to Catholicism in 1898, subsequently writing a few books on religious themes such as *The Gate of Sinners* (1908).

By 1911, the family had relocated to Hastings in Sussex. While there, Kernahan finished his autobiography, mainly composed of reminiscing about many famous people he had known e.g. Gladstone, Oscar Wilde, and Alfred Russell Wallace whose correspondence with Kernahan from Thrums can be seen at the Natural History Museum. Although this was destroyed by fire at his publishers during the 1941 bombing of London, he re-wrote it and delivered it to his publisher three months before he died!

The couple both died in Hastings, she in 1941 and he in 1943, and are buried in the borough cemetery.

But the Essex connection continued with Jeanie's son by her first marriage, George Kernahan Bettany, who moved with his wife to Canvey Island in the 1920s where they produced a monthly magazine featuring sketches and stories of their three children. In 1938 they moved to Benfleet to "a plant filled chocolate box bungalow" where she produced renowned artwork, and he wrote eleven novels, mainly westerns and adventure stories, while working for *The Spectator.* Essex features particularly prominently in *Murder in Benfleet* (1946), and it was in Essex that he died in 1949, at Southend Hospital.

(www.benfleethistory.org.uk, www.canveyisland.org)

DENISE LEVERTOV (1923 – 1977)

Denise is the first of two poets in this listing, both female, and both, coincidentally, from Ilford. (The other is Ruth Pitt.) Denise had a Welsh mother who was a teacher who read poetry to her, and her father was a multi-lingual Anglican parson although the son of a Jewish rabbi. She and her sister were home educated, and, according to the *Dictionary of Literary Biography* Denise grew up "surrounded by books and people talking about them in many languages".

Abandoning an early interest in ballet (hudsonreview.com), she moved on to poetry, and cheekily sent off a few samples to T.S.Eliot when she was twelve, receiving some "excellent advice" in return. Five years later came her first published poem — *Listening to Distant Guns*, in *Poetry Quarterly*, perhaps an unsurprising subject at the time.

During the war she became a civilian nurse in and around London, which is when she probably left Essex behind her. She did some travelling around Europe after the war, meeting her American husband-to-be, Michael Goodman, in 1947. This was a year after having her first volume of poetry published – *The Double Image*. They married and moved to New York in 1948, and their son was born a year later.

Denise became an American citizen in 1955, by which time she had also become a political activist as well as a feminist. She and her husband were active in the protest movement against the war in Vietnam, reflected in her poem *Life at War*. As her reputation grew, Denise was increasingly in demand as a lecturer and teacher and she was also the poetry editor of American publications *The Nation* in the 60s and of *Mother Jones* in the 1970s. Her volumes of poetry could be personal or political. For example, *The Sorrow Dance* (1967), reflected her opposition to the war, while *The Freeing of the Dust* (1975) alternated anti-war poems with confessional poems about her personal life. Her awards included the Shelley Memorial Award, the Robert Frost Medal, the Lannan Award, the Lenore Marshall Prize and a Guggenheim Fellowship.

She died of cancer in the U.S. leaving a legacy of more than 30 books of poetry, essays and translations. Her obituary in the *New York Times* (23rd December 1977) described her as writing "with great particularity and sensitivity about aspects of love, spiritual as well as erotic". More and more, her work conveyed her political awareness and social consciousness. She was, as in the title of her first book of essays, *The Poet in the World*. More than twenty years after her death, her last poems were published as *The Great Unknowing* on the website famouspoetsandpoems.com.

One of her poems in 1962, incidentally, reflected upon her Essex roots. This was *A Map of the Western Part of the County of Essex in England* with its references to Hainault, Clavering, Stapleford Abbotts, Woodford, and:

In Ilford High Road I saw the multitudes passing pale under
the light of flaring sundown, seven kings
in sombre starry robes gathered at Seven Kings...

WILLIAM MORRIS 1834 – 1896

While some may be surprised to see William Morris in this list, understandably given his status as a designer, he was Essex born and bred, a poet, and an author – the latter after moving out of the area. He was born in Walthamstow, when it was part of Essex and when it was rural as described in his *News from Nowhere* (1893) with its "flat pasture, once marsh … scattered red-tiled roofs and the big hayricks". A delicate child, he took to reading rather than romping (see William Addison's account in *Epping Forest*) and he moved to an even more idyllic spot when he was six.

This was Woodford Hall, a Georgian mansion, separated from the forest only by a fence, where he could ramble with his brothers on foot or on Shetland ponies.

Morris's early education was at a preparatory school in Walthamstow which moved to Woodford enabling him to continue to attend. He was one of ten siblings with a comfortable home life provided by some shrewd investing on his financier father's part. His father died in 1847 and the family moved back to Walthamstow, to a spacious house with a moat and an island, which featured in some of his later poetry.

However, according to J.W.Mackail (in *The Life of William Morris*, 1922) "He never ceased to love Epping Forest, and to uphold the scenery of his native county as beautifully and characteristically English" and Morris himself wrote of being a young man who knew the area "yard by yard from Wanstead to the Theydons and from Hale End to the Fairlop Oak." It seems that Morris's observations of birds, trees, and flowers began accumulating from those first jaunts, on his pony, around the Essex countryside, and he used them as sources for his work in pattern design.

His further education continued at Marlborough College from 1848, then Oxford to read theology, but he returned to Walthamstow during the holidays, and apparently enjoyed brass rubbing in the local churches. At Oxford he gradually veered away from the idea of holy orders to that of writing but he went on to qualify as an architect which seemed to offer better prospects. While working in London for an architectural practice, Morris not only took lessons in life drawing but he contributed a number of poems and stories to the *Oxford and Cambridge Magazine*, and had a thirty-poem volume published in 1858, *The Defence of Guinevere*, less well received. He married in 1857 and that is when he moved to Kent, to the famous red brick building which still bears his name. However, he retained a house in London, and spent considerable time in the Cotswolds where his 16th century home, Kelmscott Manor, was the inspiration for some of his earliest designs and where his friend the artist Rossetti became a bit of a fixture, potentially fixated by Morris's wife.

The Life and Death of Jason, a 13,000 line poem was published in 1867 to better reception, followed by the critically acclaimed *The Earthly*

Paradise in 1868. His growing interest in socialism and politics are reflected in his written work for the next few decades, when he was editor of the Socialist League newspaper, *The Commonweal* (until 1890), followed by another change in 1891 when Morris set up the Kelmscott Press in Hammersmith to publish limited edition illustrated books. Then came five fantasy romantic novels in his declining years, with *The Well at World's End* (for example) described as "entrancing" and "vibrant" and "imaginative" (on Amazon).

Following his death in Kelmscott House, Hammersmith, his body was taken to the Cotswolds, to Kelmscott Church. Interestingly, it was some time before his fame as a designer overtook his fame as a writer, even though his work was included in the first exhibition of the Arts and Crafts Exhibition Society in London in 1888 (where he gave a lecture on tapestry weaving). Essex's loss, maybe, but an international gain.

H. Rider Haggard had relatives living in Little Court in Stock, and the author himself visited Tiptree and Hadleigh in the early 20th century in his capacity as an agricultural expert. In Tiptree, he visited the strawberry farm where he witnessed "puggling" — a form of lifting the strawberries. In Hadleigh, he visited the Salvation Army's Home farm colony which employed unskilled labour, often from East London and who he described as "wretched men," training them to produce amazing results from unpromising soil. Haggard had already achieved success with *King Solomon's Mines* by then and went on to produce more than thirty adventure novels, as well as writing about rural England including rural Essex. His novel, *The Brethren*, set in the days of the Crusades, makes many references to St Peter's Chapel in Bradwell and Stansgate Abbey in Steeple, both near Maldon.

ARTHUR MORRISON 1863 – 1945

    Although Arthur Morrison is more closely associated with the East End of London where he was born and brought up, and which served as the background for his most famous books, he spent a couple of decades in Essex.
    The son of an engine fitter in Poplar, Morrison lost his father when he was eight (to tuberculosis), leaving his mother with three children to support. In 1879, she took on a small haberdashery shop, and he started writing comic poems for *Cycling* magazine while working as a clerk. By 1885, he was doing more journalistically, submitting "Cockney Corner" pieces to *The People* and contributing articles to *The Globe, Strand* and *National Observer*. After a few years doing clerical work for the People's Palace, an institution in Stepney bringing culture to the East End, Morrison became sub-editor of their journal *People's Palace* in 1889, and started working as a freelance in 1890 at the same time as taking on editorial work for *The Globe*.

Because of his interest in the occult, his first published book – in 1891 - was *The Shadows Around Us,* featuring supernatural tales already published in *The People*, but the editor of *National Observer* encouraged him to write about the East End slums, having become aware of Morrison's interest in social deprivation, and in his powers of description. Morrison submitted more than a dozen stories to the *National Observer,* and then collected them into *Tales of Mean Streets*, his first big hit, written after his move out of his London lodgings.

Morrison's journalistic success meant that he was able to move firstly to Chingford, on the Essex border, and then by 1896 to Salcombe House in Loughton High Road, then a rural part of Essex (a blue plaque marks the spot). Away from his writing, he had married Elizabeth who he had met at The People's Palace, and they had a son, Guy, a year later, in 1893. Two more "slum" novels were written during his time here: in 1896 came *A Child of the Jago* (a very dark and violent version of *Oliver Twist*) and in 1899 *To London Town*. He was also an early pioneer of detective fiction, and his character Horace Dorrington, in *The Dorrington Deedbox*, features in *The Golden Age of Murder* (by Martin Edwards) as the inspiration for Patricia Highsmith's *Ripley,* with his Martin Hewett detective stories as being (almost!) on a par with Conan Doyle. As for Essex, this features prominently in his *Cunning Murrell*, a study of white witchcraft in Hadleigh (1900). The writer and social historian Ken Worpole is a big fan of the *Cunning Murrell* novel, set at a time when smuggling was rife in the area; he puts it on a par with Thomas Hardy's work. His East End origins feature again in the crime novel *The Hole in The Wall* of 1902, described as "one of the minor masterpieces of this century" by classiccrimefiction.com.

Although several collections of short stories followed, Morrison began to amass Japanese and Chinese prints and began studying Oriental art, publishing a book on the subject in 1911. This brought him further financial security, but also established a level of respectability which he felt had been denied him in his earlier years – he had been reluctant to admit where he was born and brought up. His financial success took him to Arabin House in High Beach, near Epping, in 1914, an impressive Grade II listed country house, and then – after the First World War – to a mansion flat in Cavendish Square in London's West End.

During the war, his son joined the army, and Morrison served as a special constable in Essex. In this capacity, according to the *Oxford Dictionary of National Biography*, it was Morrison who phoned in the news of the first Zeppelin raid on London on Christmas Eve 1915. (The Zeppelin was shot down in the Thames estuary.)

His son died of malaria in 1921, contracted during the war, and the Morrisons moved to their last home in Chalfont St. Peter in Buckinghamshire in 1930. Apart from short fiction and articles on Oriental art, Morrison did not produce much writing in his later years. He became a freemason, was a member of the Royal Society for Literature and the Japanese Art Association.

In 1936 he presented Bethnal Green Library in the East End with the manuscript of *A Child of the Jago*, and, on his death in 1945, he left his Oriental collection of 140 paintings, plus woodcuts and ceramics, to the British Museum. The royalties of *Cunning Murrell* were bequeathed to the National Society for the Prevention of Cruelty to Children.

The report of his death in the *Evening Despatch* (5th December 1945) refers to Morrison as being of the "gifted team" including "Hardy, Kipling, Barrie and Stevenson." Quite an accolade.

The 1970s saw a mini revival of Morrison's work. Two episodes of the television series *The Rivals of Sherlock Holmes* featured Dorrington stories (with Peter Vaughan as Dorrington), and in 1977 an opera based on *A Child of the Jago* (by Shirley Thompson), was staged at the Royal Festival Hall in London.

However, much more recently (2007) The Arthur Morrison Society was formed, holding events as part of the Loughton Festival. In 2019 actor and storyteller Robert Crighton gave a reading of two of Morrison's detective stories as part of the Festival at Loughton Baptist Church, near Morrison's Loughton home.

Sir Walter Scott stayed at 'The Griffin' in Danbury, an Essex village, in 1808, where he finished the romance that Joseph Strutt (see separate chapter) left incomplete on his death. This novel, *Queenhoo Hall*, has many scenes set in Danbury, and Scott is said to have been so impressed with its success that he was encouraged to publish his own book: *Waverley* – and the rest is history! (countrylife.co.uk)

RUTH PITTER 1897 – 1992

Ruth was born in Ilford, sharing common ground with the poet Denise Levertov some years later. Similarly, she inherited a love of poetry from her parents, who were teachers in the East End of London and who held Sunday recitations of poems learned by heart. The family apparently rented "a run-down cottage without running water" in Hainault forest and she "trekked through the woods for hours with her father" (encyclopedia.com) with the cottage and the countryside appearing frequently in her poetry. This "cottage" does not seem to have been their permanent home, however, more of a holiday cottage which they did not have the money to improve.

Her first poem was published in *New Age* when she was just fourteen and still at school in East London (Coborn School in Bow, a Christian charity school), quite a distance from Ilford.

The outbreak of war meant an end to her education and she took a job in the War Office until finding something more creative: hand painting and decorating furniture for a company in Southwold on the Suffolk coast, where she met George Orwell, maintaining contact with him in later life. Ruth moved with the company to London in 1918 according to the *Oxford Dictionary of National Biography*, and stayed with them until 1930. It seems she had realised that she was not going to earn a living with her poetry even though Hilaire Belloc, the French poet, was impressed enough with her work to finance the publication of her first collections in the 1920s and 1930s.

What she did do to improve her fortunes was to then open her own business, with her friend and co-worker, Kathleen O'Hara, utilising her experience to produce painted furniture.

In her spare time, however, Ruth went on to produce another sixteen volumes of poetry in her lifetime, encompassing topics such as love, religion, nature, the human condition and ... cats. Ruth's humorous side is apparent in her choice of such subjects as earwigs or fleas! During the Blitz, the business closed and she took work in a factory, but still managed to produce a volume of poetry called *The Rude Potato,* an entertaining look at gardens and gardening.

Having moved several times before the war, mostly in and around London, she had not forgotten her Essex roots and produced a poem featuring Romford Market which appeared in *Land- marks: A Book of Topographical Verse for England and Wales* (1943):

> *With human bellow, bovine blare,*
> *Glittering trumpery, gaudy ware,*
> *The life of Romford market-square*
> *Set all our pulses pounding ...*

After the war Ruth (who never married) moved again, to Oxford, and then settled in Long Crendon in Buckinghamshire in 1952, with Kathleen. They returned to a decorative painting business – mainly trays this time.

By then she had become a close friend of C.S.Lewis who admired her work and entered into an extensive correspondence with her; and she was also praised by such luminaries as Siegfried Sassoon and Philip Larkin.

Ruth's accolades include the Hawthornden Prize for *A Trophy of Arms* in 1937 and the Heinemann Award for Literature with *The Ermine* in 1954. In 1955, she was the first woman to receive the Queen's Gold Medal for Poetry, presented by the Queen at Buckingham Palace. She was also made a Companion of Literature in 1974 and awarded a C.B.E. in 1979.

Although she turned up on radio programmes from the 40s through to the 70s, and wrote articles on gardening for *Woman* magazine, as well as continuing with her poetry, she was still decorating furniture into her seventies.

By the time she died in 1992, she had lost her sight and was disappearing into undeserved obscurity in spite of publishing another (her last) volume of poems in 1987 – *A Heaven to Find*. Let's hope she found it.

Alice Diehl (1844-1912), born in Aveley in her grandfather's house, where she spent subsequent holidays, died in Essex, in Ingatestone, having moved there not long before. But between times she seems to have lived primarily in London. Alice had piano lessons in Germany, and became a notable performer, launching in Paris in 1861, playing at the Crystal Palace in 1872, and then teaching piano. Where literature is concerned, however, she published her first book – of poems – when she was just eight, returning to writing in 1882 with her first novel, *Eve Lester*. She then wrote at least one novel a year until her death, a total of 41 altogether, plus a couple of non fiction books (on music and philosophy), with her most famous being, arguably, *Griselda* (1886) about womanly self-sacrifice. There is a plaque at her Aveley birthplace, but in between Aveley and Ingatestone she has proved difficult to track.

FRANCIS QUARLES 1592 – 1644

Francis Quarles, born in the manor house of Stewards in Romford, was a well-regarded poet, whose father was a well-to-do "Surveyor-general of Victualling for the Navy" (allpoetry.com). Orphaned by the age of fourteen, his parents were buried in Romford.

From a wealthy family, he could live a leisurely life after studying at Cambridge and Lincoln's Inn, writing religious verse and political pamphlets. He achieved the high status of cup-bearer to Princess Elizabeth (James I's daughter) in 1613 on her wedding to Frederick V, King of Bohemia from 1619, continuing his family's royal connection. In 1617 Quarles bought a house near St Paul's Cathedral and married 17-year-old Londoner, Ursula Woodgate, a year later. His first published poetry was *A Feast For Wormes* in 1620, showing men as little more than worms themselves.

Quarles was back in Essex by 1632, living at Roxwell, where he became the head of a family of eighteen children. Here he produced the most successful book of verse of the 17th century; *Emblemes* (1635) closely followed by *Hieroglyphics of the Life of Man* in 1638, almost as popular. The frontispiece of *Emblemes* shows a globe in which are inscribed the names of Essex villages Finchingfield and Roxwell, and this book with its lavish illustrations was dedicated to Edward Benlowes, a would-be-poet, wealthy virtuoso, patron, friend and Essex neighbour.

It seems Quarles moved to Terling, another Essex village, between 1638 and 1640, living at Ridley Hall, a manor house "surrounded by woodland" (quarlesfamilytree.com). While there he was appointed Chronologer of the City of London, writing a range of elegies, sonnets and prose works, often foregrounding his support for the royal family. His poetry was loved by the ordinary people "even if he was not one of them" (luminarium.org), with a great resurgence after Charles I was restored to the throne. Here is a taster from *The Shortness of Life*:

> *And what's a life? A weary pilgrimage,*
> *Whose glory in one day doth fill the stage*
> *With childhood, manhood, and decrepit age.*

Quarles died in 1644 and is buried in the parish of St Olave's in London, leaving his wife and nine surviving children in near poverty. It has been suggested that he may in fact have moved to London by then. His works remained in print for more than a century after his death, and one of his sons, John, also became an author and poet, but was exiled to Flanders as a result of his Royalist sympathies (*ODNB* Vol. 47).

RICHARD QUITTENTON 1833 – 1914

Not a name that rolls off the tongue? And nor is Roland Quiz, perhaps, his pseudonym? But Quittenton definitely merits a place among Essex authors, having spent most of his life in and around the Southend area. He understandably features in Christopher Fowler's *The Book of Forgotten Authors* (Hachette Publishing, 2017).

Although born in Lancaster, by 1907 he was living in Westcliff on Sea, having already lived in nearby Thundersley before this (per Carole Mulroney in *Leighway* magazine, January 2015, published by The Leigh Society). So he settled in Essex early on, and, according to the *Chelmsford Chronicle* (23rd January 1914), in its obituary, he later lived variously in Hockley, Southend and South Benfleet.

While editing *The Weekly Budget* (which he did for 42 years!), he wrote serial stories for its pages, which contained news and fiction, and the magazine reached a claimed circulation of 150,000 when it moved from Manchester to Fleet Street in London in 1862, doubling this figure soon after. Some of Quittenton's stories were gathered together and published as *The Budget Story Books*. One particular story was dramatized and staged in London: *Belle Vue*. In 1871, *Our Young Folks Weekly Budget* began as a spin off from *The Weekly Budget*, a weekly magazine for children which went through a number of name changes, and Quittenton was again a prolific contributor. He became joint editor and wrote humorous sketches, rhymes and children's stories as well as what Christopher Fowler calls "blood and thunder adventures" for older readers (*The Independent* 18th October 2013). The magazine's motto was "To Inform, To Instruct, To Amuse" and it was the longest running of its Victorian rivals (until 1897).

Additionally, Quittenton wrote a book set in his Lancashire roots, *A Mystery of the Lane,* (according to the *Chronicle*) but became well known at the time for his four Tim Pippin children's books which started life in *Young Folks.* He used the pseudonym Roland Quiz, with these books first published in 1874 but continually reprinted until after the Second World War. One of these, *Giant Land*, followed the trend in many Victorian children's stories, featuring a nightmarish image of "Uncle Two-Heads sinking into the quicksand" – cosy they were not. Tiny Tim faced such memorable villains as the Giant Body Snatcher, the Hassidic Giant Greed (clearly anti-semitic) and Queen Mab, all disturbingly illustrated (by "Puck").

Quittenton seems to have been well travelled, and counted Charles Dickens and Robert Louis Stevenson among his friends. He was a freemason, a forester who married twice, producing 21 children, only five of whom were still alive at the time of his death. He was also on the lecture circuit, with a report of one lecture "at Hullbridge" in November 1894 about the Poor Law System drawing a "numerous audience" (*Essex Herald* 4th December 1894).

He was still writing in his 81st year although his sight was failing but died shortly before Christmas 1914 at his home in South Benfleet following a bout of pleurisy and bronchitis. The funeral took place at Sutton Cemetery in Southend, where he was buried beside his wife who had pre-deceased him by two years. The books of Roland Quiz still turn up on such sites as abebooks but his image has proved elusive.

Ian Fleming was a member of the Naval Intelligence Service and on Whitsun Saturday afternoon 1940, he and his brother Peter (an Assistant in Military Intelligence) drove in a camouflaged staff car to Southend-on-Sea as a result of the threat of an attack threatened for the following day, where they joined a naval observation post on the roof of the Palace Hotel – standing prominently at the shore end of Southend's famous pier. Their undercover task was to report back any sign of an impending enemy attack, but by the early hours of the morning, with no indication of enemy aircraft movement, they gave up and arranged for their driver to take them back to the capital! Years later, Fleming had become a friend of the wealthy Ivar Bryce (related to the Mountbattens) and visited him at his Essex mansion, Moyns Park in Birdbrook, North Essex. This was at the end of the 1950s and it was rumoured that he finished the final draft of *From Russia With Love* while there.

RUTH RENDELL 1930 – 2015

This author is probably the most famous Essex writer of all. She was born in South Woodford (before it was swallowed up by Greater London), an only child, both parents being teachers. Her eccentric Swedish mother and mathematical father were polar opposites, making for a less than happy childhood, further complicated by her mother's deterioration into multiple sclerosis when Ruth was very young, leaving her to be brought up by the housekeeper. But, at age seven, she first walked into a public library, her "entrance into books" (*East Anglian Daily Times* 2nd May 2015).

The family moved to Loughton shortly before Ruth started her main education at the County High School for Girls there, although her education was interrupted by evacuation to the Cotswolds in 1942. When she left school she became a feature writer for the *Chigwell Times* becoming top reporter there by the age of 22. While covering an inquest she met Don Rendell, a fellow journalist (on the *Stratford and Newham Express*), and they married at St Mary's, Loughton, on 18 March 1950. According to the *East Anglian Daily Times*, early married life was spent in Leyton, East London, a few miles from the Essex border, but she "didn't care for the area at all" and this is probably why she did not talk about her East London experiences during interviews.

It seems she had several novels rejected during the 1950s, but finally, in 1964, *From Doon With Death* was accepted by John Long, with a payment of £75. This introduced Chief Inspector Reginald Wexford, who featured in twenty-three further novels (in the last two, *The Vault* and *No Man's Nightingale*, he had retired) as well as in several short stories. The phenomenal success of the Wexford novels was partly due to the fact that he was "down to earth, big, bluff, self-educated, working to provide for his family and living in a modest house in the suburbs of a small town" and partly due to Ruth's use of character and psychology rather than reliance on police procedure.

The couple were soon in a position to move to bigger and better houses, and she moved eighteen times during her lifetime, with many of those years spent in Suffolk, a county she grew very fond of. For several years, she lived in a pink 16th-century manor house set in 11 acres but she also found herself able to have a rural retreat in Suffolk as well as a comfortable home in London. (In several interviews in the 2010s for instance, she was living in Little Venice.)

Ruth divorced Don in 1975 but they re-married in 1977 – in *The Guardian*'s obituary (2nd May 2015) she revealed that "after they separated, she found she couldn't live without him."

By the mid 1980s, apart from writing a number of stand-alone crime novels, she had started on a series of fourteen books under the name Barbara Vine. These were much darker and more chilling, with no bluff officer to offer reassurances of redemption or salvation, as affirmed by www.britishcouncil.org. They were psychological thrillers in the main, featuring ordinary people pushed to the brink; but she did not dwell on blood and violence. Not only that but she wrote three novellas, produced ten collections of short stories, some of which had been sold individually to U.S. publications such as *Ellery Queen Mystery Magazine*, and even a children's book; *Archie & Archie* (2013).

In all, Ruth published eighty books, selling more than 20,000,000 copies in 33 languages. *The Epping Forest Guardian* (5th May 2015), refers to the use of Epping Forest and Loughton in some of her fiction, with particular reference to *The Face of Trespass* (1974) where she referred to the hilly part of Loughton as Little Cornwall.

Many of her books were adapted into television dramas and films. Between 1987 and 2000, ITV broadcast *The Ruth Rendell Mysteries*, the first half dozen series featuring Inspector Wexford, played by George Baker, with later series adapting stand-alone novels and short stories. Nine feature films were based on her novels, several of them French including her favourite, Chabrol's *La Ceremonie* (1995), based on *A Judgement in Stone*. This has been hailed on such forums as theconflictedfilmsnob.com as "a sharp commentary on class difference rather than a tale of murder" – a not unusual subject for Ruth Rendell.

As a result of the popularity of her work, she received numerous awards: three Edgars from The Mystery Writers of America, three Daggers from the British Crimewriters' Association, the Arts Council National Book Award, *The Sunday Times* Award for Literary Excellence, and became a CBE in 1996 and Baroness Rendell of Babergh of Aldeburgh in Suffolk in 1997! Aside from her prolific written output, Ruth was an active Labour Peer in the House of Lords, a supporter of the Campaign for Nuclear Disarmament, a lifelong feminist (who, for example, did not like the title 'Queen of Crime' regarding it as sexist). She was also a generous supporter of various charities including Shelter, the National Literacy Trust, Little Hearts Matter, Kids for Kids, and an ambassador for The Stroke Association – ironically perhaps as that is how she died: in St George's Hospital, South London, following a second stroke.

During her final years, as a widow in her 80s, with a housekeeper for company at her London home, Ruth continued writing. Her last Wexford novel was *No Man's Nightingale* in 2013, and a year later she created a new detective, Colin Quell, for *The Girl Next Door*, set in Loughton, on the edge of Epping Forest. It seems she had come full circle, compounded by the arrival of her son, Simon (aged 62), in February 2016 when he travelled from his home in Colorado to be at the unveiling of a blue plaque on her Loughton home.

Ernest Laurie-Long 1886-1969: This prolific novelist, with around seventy nautical novels to his name, was born in North London but appears in 1907 on marriage records in Rochford when he married Ethel. According to rochforddistricthistory.org.uk he was living in Eastwood Road, Rayleigh in 1911, although listed as an "umbrella manufacturer" – a way of earning a living before achieving success as an author perhaps. While he was known to have served in the First World War, in the RAMC, there are no Essex references until his name appears as living before the Second World War "for some years at Gidea Park" in a booklet produced by the London Borough of Havering entitled *South Essex Authors* issued for National Library Week 1966. Information on his books is more readily available, his first being in 1934 (*Port of Destination*) and his last in 1964 (*In Full Commission*), with more than sixty in between, with hundreds of reviews on the British Newspaper Archives, describing them, variously, as "rollicking" or "exciting" or "thrilling" or "swashbuckling" etc. Of these, twelve feature Captain Flynn, and these seem to have been particularly popular. Laurie-Long died in Suffolk in 1969, but his books, and his mystery, linger on.

DOROTHY L. SAYERS 1893 – 1957

Born in Oxford to a solicitor's daughter and a clergyman, this might be the ideal combination for someone interested in crime and theology. The family moved into a spacious but spartan Georgian rectory in a remote part of East Anglia in 1897 close to the River Ouse. As a child, Dorothy learned Latin and French, mainly through home tuition, and won a scholarship to the Oxford women's college, Somerville, in 1912, earning an M.A. in 1920 as one of the first female Oxford graduates.

The 1920s, the decade before she moved to Essex, were pretty eventful for Dorothy. She was a teacher in Yorkshire and in France, a reader for an Oxford publishers, and worked for an advertising agency (Benson's) where she penned the slogan "My Goodness, My Guinness". She also had an illegitimate son, fathered by a car salesman and brought up by her cousin. After several unsuitable "crushes", she married journalist Oswald Fleming in 1926, a man known to suffer from the effects of his First World War experiences. From 1921-1929 she was living in Great James Street in central London. Plenty of material there for several novels!

However, she was writing poetry (two volumes were published) and translating other writers' work during the 1920s, although she wanted to write detective novels – and managed to find a publisher for her first Lord Peter Wimsey novel in 1923: *Whose Body*?

Dorothy moved to Witham, near Chelmsford in Essex, in 1929, the year she founded the Detection Club (with the likes of Agatha Christie), following the publication of another three Wimsey novels, with another seven to follow in the early 1930s. These novels, among those of the Golden Age of Mystery, showed her interest in social history, anarchy, consumption and waste in the modern world (*Murder must Advertise*), the situation of women, the devastating effects of war (*The Unpleasantness at the Bellona Club*), the meaning of work, the arguments between science and religion, and the implications of the class system. (For a full analysis of all Wimsey books see the *Oxford Dictionary of National Biography*.) One anonymous on-line quote says that she made Wimsey "a rich aristocrat so that she might have the fun of spending his fortune", an interesting summation.

The Nine Tailors from 1934, set in the Cambridgeshire Fens of her childhood, was included in the 1987 volume of *Crime and Mystery: The 100 Best Books,* authored by H.R.F.Keating. The first screening of Wimsey was a black and white adaptation of a short story *The Silent Passenger* (1935) for which she wrote the scenario but seems to have thought that the final version was a "travesty" (wordpress.com). Maybe this was one of many reasons why she wrote no more Wimsey novels after 1937 although she did follow up with three collections of short stories featuring her popular detective.

Witham was her home for nearly thirty years, but, while settled domestically, she moved away from her successful detective novels to writing for the theatre and radio. She was also responsible for such academic works as *Letters to a Diminished Church* and *Are Women Human?* and wrote a number of literary reviews in the 1930s for *The Sunday Times* as well as renowned theological essays.

Busman's Honeymoon in 1935 was a play before it became her last Wimsey novel, but other plays were mainly religious dramas. One successful example was *The Man Born To Be King*, a series of twelve radio plays about the life of Christ on BBC radio transmitted during the Second World War. It was 1942 when the *Chelmsford Chronicle* mentioned her giving lectures to the troops (2nd October), leaving her less time for her writing.

Away from her books, she became an Honorary Life Member of the Essex Association of Change [Bell] Ringers in 1950 (*Chelmsford Chronicle* 3rd November, 1950) and gave lectures in and around Essex on the freedom of the press. Described as "large of body and of heart" by the ODNB, she was also described by *The Guardian* as a proficient motor cyclist (22nd July 2008), so obviously a woman of diverse character and interests.

She was working on a major translation of Dante's *Divine Comedy* at the time of her sudden unexpected death, at home, in 1957, seven years after being widowed. Interestingly, having been a churchwarden at St. Anne's in Soho when living in London, she wanted to be buried there although the church was bombed in World War II. Her ashes are interred beneath the tower, which was left standing by the bombs.

The story of Dorothy L. Sayers does not end here. There was a Lord Peter Wimsey television series from 1972-1975 featuring Ian Carmichael as Wimsey, and there were further television adaptations in 1987 with Edward Petherbridge. In 1988, an uncompleted Wimsey novel (*Thrones, Dominations*) was finished by Jill Paton Walsh, becoming an immediate best-seller. There is a statue opposite her former home, a collection of her work at the nearby Dorothy L. Sayers Centre, and continued interest via the Dorothy L. Sayers Society, founded in 1976, which publishes collections of her letters, etc. Essex – be proud!

DODIE SMITH 1896 – 1990

While Dodie Smith did not turn up in Essex until 1934, she spent most of the rest of her life there. But to start at the beginning, this was in Whitfield Lancashire, until her father died when she was two, meaning a move to Manchester to live with grandparents, uncles and aunts. Another move came in 1910 when her mother remarried, this time to London, where she auditioned a few years later for the Royal Academy of Dramatic Art, aiming to become an actress.

However, she got sacked from her first job in a musical comedy, paying £2 per week, and struggled to make a living with end-of-pier farces and army concert parties while living in a girls' hostel in London (*The Illustrated London News,* 1st February 1976).

Rather than continue playing parlour maids and to improve her finances she switched to running the art gallery at Heals, the furniture shop, and found she enjoyed selling and travelling to buy goods for the store. But she also tried her hand at writing – a play called *Autumn Crocus* written on a typewriter gifted by her boss (and lover!) at Heals. This she sold to director Basil Dean, someone she had met when he was an actor. Her fee was £100 and the play's success inspired such headlines as "Shopwoman Dramatist ... Hit of the Season" in the *London Daily News* (8th April 1931). It ran for a year in the West End, making her rich pretty much overnight, and was later filmed, inspiring her to write a succession of light comedies in the 1930s, with *Dear Octopus* (1938) starring John Gielgud, being her biggest triumph. This ran for two years and secured its place in repertory for the next 60 years!

At the height of her fame, just before leaving Heals in 1933, Dodie bought a flat in Dorset Square, and two years later (additionally) a large thatched cottage in rural Finchingfield - for £435! (thecritic.co.uk). She had teamed up by then with another Heals employee, Alec Beesley, seven years her junior, who became her manager and general factotum, and she had also acquired her first dalmatian, Pongo, bought by Alec as a birthday gift. Pongo was the first of nine dalmatians in Dodie's life.

Her 1935 play *Call It a Day* ran for 509 performances in London and a further 194 nights on Broadway, before transferring to the silver screen with Olivia de Havilland, making it her most successful in financial terms. While her plays continued to be produced, the couple decided to leave for the United States as the Second World War loomed (*ODNB*), partly because Alec was a conscientious objector. They married in the U.S. in 1940 and spent thirteen years there, mainly in Hollywood, because Dodie was in constant demand at the studios to re-write screenplays and to work on a new play (*Lovers and Friends*, 1942). She wrote her first novel, *I Capture the Castle,* while there, and was awarded with rave reviews, e.g.

The Marylebone Mercury (8th April 1949) regarding it as a "triumph" for her in this "new medium," and describing the story, featuring a 17 year old girl in the wilds of Suffolk, as "out of the ordinary … escapist literature."

The couple returned to their cottage in 1953, but this was not a good time for playwrights unless they were producing kitchen sink dramas. So, unusually, she had two flops and more than a half dozen plays that were not even produced, although *Dear Octopus* was revived in 1968. But in the meantime, of course, came *101 Dalmatians*, published in 1956. This was inspired by a passing comment years before by a friend who thought Pongo would make a good fur coat, and partly perhaps reinforced by the décor of the London flat which was monochrome – white carpets with black curtains (very Cruella de Vil).

Walt Disney showed immediate interest and snapped up the film rights, turning Cruella into No. 3 of the Top 10 Disney All Time Villains (though she is even more cruel in the book than the films of 1961 and 1996). Cruella's home, Hell Hall, is said to be based on Greys Hall in Sible Hedingham, a large listed period property some seven miles from Finchingfield. It is certainly very different from Dodie's cottage described as having "idyllic charm" with its "doves and honeysuckle" (*Illustrated London News*, above). According to this same feature, when Disney visited her home to discuss the film rights of *I Capture the Castle*, she told him she wanted four times what he paid for *101 Dalmatians*, but they compromised with a figure in the middle.

She wrote another five novels, two children's books, and four autobiographical volumes in her remaining years, continuing after her husband died in 1987. *Look Back with Love* - one of her memoirs – was arguably the most successful of these. Dodie ended her days in her beloved Finchingfield, which has a plaque on the cottage, and she was cremated there, her ashes scattered on the wind. In her will, she left £2,000 to Charley, the last of her beloved dalmatians.

Her correspondence with friends such as John Gielgud and Christopher Isherwood (a regular visitor to the cottage) are archived at Boston University in the U.S.A. In 2003, *I Capture the Castle* was also turned into a film, with Bill Nighy, having sold several million copies, not far behind the sales of *101 Dalmatians*. However, perhaps Dodie should be remembered as one of our most successful playwrights even though her fame lies with just a couple of her novels.

SUSAN SMYTHIES c.1720 – c.1790?

Susan Smythies may have only written four books but a) she is an Essex girl through and through, and b) even to have three books published in the 18th century by a woman was worthy of recognition. Few women had managed this before Susan, and it was another 100 years before such as Jane Austen and the Bronte sisters finally gave women real, if limited, opportunities in the field.

She was born in Colchester to the local rector/teacher and his first wife, and was part of a large family with at least six siblings. Her mother's inscription on the family vault in Mile End Churchyard refers to her as the mother of ten, seven of which survived. Tracing Susan's early life and education has proved elusive, but her writings show that she was well versed in the work of such greats as her contemporary peers who were regarded as the founders of the traditional English novel: Henry Fielding and Samuel Richardson. Although it seems she was personally known to Richardson, all that is known about her private life is that she was unmarried!

Susan's first book was *The Stage-coach*, published anonymously (of course) in 1753 with five further volumes in 1755 and 1789. This gave the stories of passengers travelling from Scarborough to London, and was unusual in having the stage-coach at the heart of the story rather than a main protagonist. *The History of Lucy Wellers*, which ran to just two volumes, was published in 1754 and 1755. It was about a servant girl who ends up rich and was translated into French and German. The French translation praises the work in its introduction. Her last adult novel, also in two volumes, was *The Brothers* (1758 and 1759), about a young woman coerced into becoming a "gentleman's" mistress but ending up with someone more eligible and wealthy.

It seems she hoped this novel would do as well as Richardson's *Clarissa,* but it was not to be as she struggled to find a publisher. Instead she opted, on Richardson's advice, to promote the book by private subscription, and ended up with 675 subscribers, mainly from Essex, with some as far afield as Cambridge and Oxford, and including Richardson. Susan was obviously pleased with this result because she published a thankyou letter in the *Ipswich Journal* in October 1758. (*Oxford Dictionary of National Biography*).

Incidentally, she makes a reference to Aphra Behn's novels in *The Brothers* – Behn being one of the few women who achieved some acclaim for her work, mainly plays, 100 years before Susan.

A children's book was credited to her *c.1798* – *The History of a Pin, as Related by Itself*. It seems that this could have been published after her death, because the date of her death has not been established by the various historians who have shown an interest in foregrounding Susan's story. The general consensus is that she was still alive in 1776 when her father died, because he left her £100 in his will plus an annuity, the bulk of his estate divided between his sons (archive.org).

An elusive, shadowy figure, she would have been amazed to see that her books, 300 years later, can be bought from specialist shops for hundreds of pounds each.

Marjorie Warby 1898-1997: This romantic Mills and Boon novelist has proved the most elusive of all. According to the London Borough of Havering's list of *South Essex Authors* in 1966, she was then a resident of Upminster. Further research shows that she was born in North London, but died in Southend on Sea. The usual sources of information for Upminster and Southend-on-Sea have proved ineffectual in finding out more about this, in her time, popular novelist. She wrote 23 novels between 1933 and 1992, starting with Mills and Boon and moving to Collins in 1941. In 1938, she was listed in The Most Popular Twopenny Library Authors as one of the 68 in the Love and Romance category, and she also had a number of stories serialised in *Woman's Weekly*, often set in exotic locations, popular in the 1940s and 1950s particularly, e.g. a heroine travelling to a coffee plantation in Kenya in *Foolish Heart* and another taking on the role of a governess in Uganda in *Comfortable Home Offered*. While there is plenty about her books in the British Newspaper Archive and other sources, Margery remains a bit of a mystery – the only other Essex reference found was her attendance at the Brentwood Writers Circle in December 1950 where she described her willingness to help members. (*Brentwood Gazette* 9th December 1950)

JOSEPH STRUTT 1749 - 1802

Joseph Strutt, a miller's son, was born in Chelmsford in 1749 at Mill House, adjacent to Springfield Mill (now a listed building). This Essex boy was educated at the King Edward VI Grammar School, where a school "house" is named in his honour. At the age of 14, he was apprenticed to an engraver in London where he was a star pupil and became a well-regarded artist, antiquarian and engraver, and he moved to the capital in 1774, having divided his time in the years before between London and Chelmsford.

His engravings became the main thrust of the handful of books he produced, books on a grand and memorable scale. The first, in 1773, was **The Regal and Ecclesiastical Antiquities of England**, essentially a series of engraved portraits, illustrative of the English monarchs, emphasising the importance of accuracy in representing historic dress in artworks. Between 1774 and 1776 Strutt published three volumes of *Manners, Customs, Arms, Habits etc. of the People of England*, followed by the two volumes of his *Chronicle of England*, (1777-8) all profusely illustrated, and involving a vast amount of research. In 1778, after his wife died in childbirth, he concentrated for some time on his artwork. Annual summer holidays to Bocking (where his wife came from) stopped at this point, so he was lost to Essex. However, his best work, in literary terms, was yet to come.

In 1801 came Strutt's most important and famous book *The Sports and Pastimes of the People of England* with over 400 pages illustrated with 140 of his engravings. Legend has it that the book, his most successful, influenced the revival of the modern Olympic Games. While this may be true, his conclusion that football had "fallen into disrepute and is but little practised" showed his summations were not always predictable. The book has hardly been out of print since. Among the "past-times" included, incidentally, is a fascinating game called Hot Cockles, popular at Christmas, apparently, which involved placing your head in someone's lap while guessing who was hitting you from behind. Strutt's research was certainly all-encompassing.

Strutt died in 1802 and was buried at St Andrews, Holborn. However, his grave is one of a large number that were subsequently re-interred at Manor Park, when the Holborn Viaduct was constructed. This means that he is buried, perhaps ironically, just a short distance away from the 2012 London Olympic Park. A blue plaque in his memory was erected at his home, in Victoria Road, Chelmsford in – appropriately – 2012. He may not have produced many books but those he did produce were significant and transformative, as were his engravings and artwork.

THE TAYLORS
JANE 1783 – 1824, ANN 1782 – 1866, JEFFERYS 1792 – 1853

This literary family spent many years in Ongar and Colchester. They moved to Colchester from Suffolk in 1796 when the father, Revd Isaac (a part time writer and engraver) moved to a nonconformist church there, with his wife Ann, a children's writer, along with their five surviving children (six died in infancy). The eldest children, Jane and Ann, formed a literary circle in the town, meaning that they were obliged to produce a piece of poetry or prose every month, although they had been fond of poetry long before this, with Jane apparently standing on the counter in the local baker's shop in Lavenham, Suffolk, reciting nursery rhymes!

Ann became the first to be published in 1798 when she was sixteen. This was a poem in the *Minor's Pocket Book* and she continued to make contributions to the same journal for thirteen years. One of the poems published in these pages was *Crippled Child's Complaint*, drawing on the lameness of her brother Jefferys, who also became a writer for children.

Jane's first poem was published in 1804, *The Beggar Boy*, resulting in the sisters being invited to be the major contributors to *Original Poems for Infant Minds* (1804) which did well enough to be translated into four other languages and ran to fifty editions. This success was followed in 1806 by *Rhymes for the Nursery*, which featured Jane's most famous rhyme *Twinkle, Twinkle, Little Star*. The girls went on to produce three more books of poems for children, often including their own engravings, having been taught by their father.

Revd Isaac was moved on again, to Ongar, in 1811 and stayed with the chapel there until his death in 1829. The family lived first at Castle House, an impressive moated grange, and then at Peaked Farm from 1814, close to Epping Forest. Father Isaac and mother Ann both had books published during their years in Ongar, while Isaac Junior earned a name for his illustrations and miniatures.

When Isaac Junior moved to Devon early in 1813 for health reasons, Ann and Jane accompanied him, Ann moving to Yorkshire when she married the Revd Joseph Gilbert at the end of 1813, ending the sisters' collaboration. They had had more poems published jointly than individually. Ann in any case became busy raising eight children of her own. While in Devon, though, Jane completed two more volumes of poetry.

In William Addison's book about *Epping Forest*, he sums up Ann's poetry as "sociable and practical", and Jane's as "sensitive, shy and mercurial." More famously, Robert Browning considered Jane's poems "the most perfect things of their kind in the English language" and described her as "noble … and imaginative." [go.gale.com]

When Jane was diagnosed with breast cancer in 1822 she moved back to be with her parents in Ongar, now living in a smaller house on the outskirts, with brother Isaac living a few miles away in Stanford Rivers. By then she had produced a final series of essays for the *Youth's Magazine*. She died in 1824 and was buried in her father's church. Ann died in Nottingham in 1866, although she is known to have visited Isaac Junior in 1853, a year after she was widowed. Isaac Junior, incidentally, not to be outdone, had authored *Natural History of Enthusiasm* in 1829 when at Stanford Rivers.

Brother Jefferys was educated at Brentwood, unlike his older sisters, being born in 1792, and settled in later life at Pilgrim's Hatch nearby. He published seventeen books for children in his lifetime e.g. *Harry's Holiday*, *The Barn and the Steeple*, and *Aesop in Rhyme.*

T.E.Lawrence (yes, Lawrence of Arabia, but also the author of a handful of popular books based on his personal experiences before and during the Arab revolt) bought 18 acres of land at Chingford's highest point, Pole Hill in 1919 – when Chingford was in Essex. According to the local *Guardian* (19 November 2016) he imagined the peaceful area as an ideal place to set up a private press to print fine-edition books. He had planned to build a house there, but this never materialised although he did have a hut and a swimming pool built (!) which he visited, and he eventually sold the land after the First World War to the Conservators of Epping Forest so it would not be developed. It is said that Lawrence burned his second draft of *Seven Pillars of Wisdom* in a bonfire on the hill, although this was of course eventually – and famously - published, in 1926. Apparently the hut was removed in 1930 and re-erected in The Warren, Loughton, but a plaque remains at Pole Hill.

H.G. WELLS 1866 – 1946

Born in Bromley, Kent, Wells attended one of the Victorian dame schools nearby until enrolling at the privately owned Bromley Academy for the sons of tradesmen (his father was a shopkeeper – and a professional cricketer). Although a star pupil, his parents struggled with the fees and he tried a series of jobs, ending up as a pupil teacher in Kensington at the Normal School of Science. His studies continued, but were overtaken by his love of reading for pleasure, and it is some years later when he turns up in Essex.

His earliest published work was a comic strip *The Desert Daisy* (1857) and he founded the *Science Schools' Journal* while at The Normal School. His next teaching post was in Wales, where he contracted tuberculosis, progressing – once he had his B.Sc. – to rather more prestigious schools in London. Although having some minor success with articles in the educational press, his health meant he was forced into trying freelance journalism, supported by his wife Isabel, a cousin he had married in 1891. (ODNB).

This was the making of Wells, who had a lot more success with short stories and essays, culminating in *The Time Machine* in 1895, what we would now call a best-seller. This was followed in quick succession by *The Island of Doctor Moreau* (1896), *The Invisible Man* (1897), and *The War of the Worlds* (1898), the latter prominently featuring the Essex coastline with its references to local areas. He refers, for instance, to the appearance of a Martian "small and faint in the remote distance, advancing along the muddy coast from the direction of Foulness". This was as the Martians "passed through Tillingham." Many other Essex villages are mentioned, including Maldon, Harwich, Walton, Clacton, Shoeburyness, Chipping Ongar, Colchester and Epping. He continued to produce novels on an annual basis, some semi-autobiographical, some described as "scientific romances."

By 1895 Wells had divorced his first wife and married one of his students, Amy, known as Jane. They moved to Sandgate in Kent for the benefit of his health, then back to London in 1909, but they appear in Essex from 1910. Wells had met the Countess of Warwick a few years earlier as they were both members of the Fabian Society, and he moved into the Little Easton Rectory on her estate at Great Easton near Dunmow (known as Easton Glebe), which had been empty for some years, while retaining a London address.

This home, surrounded by woodland and gardens, proved an ideal spot for Wells' young family (he and Jane had two young sons by then), and offered Wells peace and quiet on the one hand and a superior social circle on the other. Daisy Greville, the Countess of Warwick, introduced Wells to her connections, and these, along with his literary connections, meant a stream of well known visitors, lavishly entertained by Wells who enjoyed parties, charades and every kind of outdoor game.

The novelist and feminist Rebecca West, who became more than just "a guest" at Easton Glebe, had met Wells (27 years her senior) in 1912, and she became one of his longer-standing mistresses. Jane, it seems, turned a blind eye to his many affairs.

Young Rebecca gave birth to Wells's son, Anthony, in 1914. Three years later mother and son moved from Great Easton into a house overlooking the estuary at Leigh on Sea. It was certainly more convenient than another property suggested by Wells at Hunstanton in Norfolk. It seems that Anthony enjoyed living at the "seaside" close to gardens, bowling greens and parks. That is, until the Zeppelins overhead drove them to return to London in 1919, and the relationship between Wells and West came under too much strain for them to continue after 1920.

Soon after this, Wells's son Frank became interested in architectural design and oversaw the construction of a garden study in the Glebe garden, which is where Wells did all of his writing from around 1920. According to Felice Spurrier, writing in *Beyond The Forest* in 1986 from memory (Five Parishes Publications) Wells was a great disciplinarian where his writing was concerned, allowing "no diversion". During this period, he was converted to full-blown socialism, perhaps surprisingly by Lady Warwick, who hosted meetings of trade unionists at her home, Easton Lodge. Certainly his output during the years of the First World War was far more political – e.g. *The War that will End War* (1914) and *Mr Britling Sees it Through* (1916), the latter based on life at Little Easton during the First World War with the name of the village changed to Matching's Easy. Earlier books, incidentally, had made good use of his early experiences in the world of work and of near-poverty, with a comic twist. For instance, *Kipps* (1905) and *The History of Mr Polly* (1910) utilised his experiences working in a drapers', and were both, incidentally, turned into films.

Wells' wife Jane was an indispensable ally, typing all his manuscripts, helping to correct proofs and involved in research for much more serious works as *Outline of History*, a 'Plain History of Life and Mankind' (1920), which became a surprising hit.

Life at Easton Glebe, however, was not all work. George Bernard Shaw, a frequent guest, produced an amateur version of *The Taming of the Shrew* in Lady Warwick's Barn Theatre close by in 1920, with the cast coached by Ellen Terry, no less, known to the Countess. Other established regulars were Arnold Bennett, Henry James, Somerset Maugham, G.K.Chesterton, Joseph Conrad, and the actress Elsa Lanchester, with Charlie Chaplin at one point on the guest list.

Everyone attending the Wells' popular dinner parties had to argue for their supper, with no intellectual holds barred. He was also involved with Lady Warwick's introduction of a summer school at Easton Lodge, putting the house and its accommodation – with its tennis courts, swimming pool, library and lecture theatre - at the disposal of the local Educational Fellowship (founded jointly with Wells in 1921).

Sadly, following a lecture at the Sorbonne in Paris in 1927, where he was joined by his wife, Jane was diagnosed with cancer. He quickly returned from Paris to Easton Glebe and stayed with her for her final six months. She died the same day that their son Frank was married, and Wells was deeply affected as can be seen by his preface to a book he later published called *The Book of Catherine Wells* (Catherine was her middle name) featuring her own writing: "I do not know what I would have done without her."

He continued at Easton Glebe for another three years, then moved to London, managing to continue writing without Jane through the Second World War until his death soon after (August 1946) at his Regents Park flat. Just a year before, two rather diverse books had been produced: *Mind at the End of its Tether* (a bleak vision of the future, cementing his record as the father of science fiction writing) and *The Happy Turning,* both portraying human inadequacies in the wake of the war. In total, 141 books appeared with H.G. Wells as the author.

When the rector of Little Easton, R.L. Gwynne, published a history of the parish in 1923, Wells contributed the preface. All in all, quite a legacy and yet another Essex author "honoured" in the Wills's Famous British Authors cigarette cards in the 1930s.

JAMES WENTWORTH DAY 1899-1983

Although born in Suffolk, Day ended his days in Ingatestone in a house called Peacocks full of treasures from his extensive travels. His literary career (as journalist and author) resulted in over forty books about East Anglia, about ghosts, royalty, sport, dogs, fishing and nature, culminating in his *Book of Essex* in 1979, well-thumbed by subsequent Essex historians. He also contributed to *The Field, Country Life, East Anglian* and *Saturday Review* where he was able to air his views on the positivity of the Agrarian lifestyle.

According to Ingatestone resident Robert Fletcher, Day was a regular at the Star Inn in his later years, although it has been tricky to pin down the exact date he actually moved there. However, there are references to him in local papers as far back as the *Chelmsford Chronicle* of the 9th December 1949 being "of Ingatestone" when he attempted without success to become the Tory M.P. for Hornchurch, so Ingatestone certainly seems to have been a long-term residence.

Farming Adventure described his rides around the farms of East Anglia on horseback during World War Two, although he spent much of this war working as a war correspondent for the BBC until being invalided home in 1943, the year the book was published. A decade later he created some controversy with his views on homosexuality and mixed marriage when being interviewed by Daniel Farsons, leading to his being frozen out of these interviews (which can still be viewed on Youtube and via the B.F.I.)

Historian and author L.E.Jerram-Burrows writes fondly of Day in her 1993 book *Smuggler's Moon*, having met him four years before his death by which time Day was totally blind and had been dictating his work since his sight began to fail. She describes his love of the islands of South Essex: Wallasea, Potton and Foulness. It seems that this is where he spent time with his (third) wife enjoying the peace and solitude that could be found there as well as pursuing his favourite sport of wild-fowling. They "got to know the islanders well and formed many lasting friendships." In her book, she describes Day's love for these islands as inspiring him to write "in a style so delicate and natural that his delightfully descriptive passages are today among our literary treasures."

R.D. WINGFIELD 1928 – 2007

Pictured on his wedding day, Rodney David Wingfield, to give him his full (though mainly unused!) names, was one of many born in the East End who moved to Essex in later life. His story starts in Hackney, but he was living in Pitsea from 1971 and just a few miles further, Basildon, a year later. If you don't recognise his name, you will certainly recognise the name Jack Frost, the detective that featured in his novels, and the spin-off television series, *A Touch of Frost*.

Wingfield was evacuated from the East End during World War Two (his father was killed in the Blitz) but returned to attend Coopers School in Bow (the school also moved to Essex i.e. to Upminster in 1971), avoiding National Service because of his poor eyesight. His working life began doing clerical work in a series of East End companies, including the Fina Oil Company, where he met his wife Phyllis: they married in 1953.

By the 1960s he was starting to write short plays in his spare time, finally having one accepted by the BBC in 1968. This was *Compensating Error*, set in the familiar surrounds of an office. This first play led to a commission for two more, and they were all so well-received that he felt confident enough to give up his job to concentrate on playwriting. By 1987, forty dramas had been produced by Radio Four, the vast majority being 45-60 minute crime mysteries with clever twists and surprise endings (some with pseudonyms). Wingfield also tried his hand at comedy, writing scripts for Kenneth Williams, but found him difficult to work with, and he did not repeat the experience.

Quite early on in his writing career, he was approached by the publishers Macmillan who offered him a £50 advance for a crime novel (in 1972). This was *Frost at Christmas* but was promptly rejected, no doubt in part because of its verbosity: it ran to 250,000 words. However, Wingfield's agent finally found a home for the novel in Canada in 1984, with publication in the U.K. following in 1989. In the meantime, two of his radio plays recycled the shambling detective: *Three Days of Frost* was produced in 1977 and *A Touch of Frost* in 1992. The latter became Wingfield's second novel, and three more Frost novels followed in the 1990s – *Night Frost, Hard Frost* and *Winter Frost,* with *A Killing Frost* published in 2008 after his death.

The author and reviewer Mike Ripley was a particular fan of the Frost books. He felt that Frost seemed "remarkably like many of the real CID detectives in West London I knew… or at least a middle-age version of them. Here was a policeman you might not like, but it was a character anyone … could recognise as an ordinary bloke doing a particularly unpleasant job." When *A Touch of Frost* was published in 1990 by Constable, he got a chance to review it for *The Sunday Telegraph* and raved that it was "altogether a funny, frantic, utterly refreshing brew" (See shotsmag.co.uk). He was not the only fan. Wingfield acquired international fame and was popular in the U.S. and Japan, with his novels translated into eleven languages, in spite of the fact that Wingfield did not find writing novels that easy: he preferred playwriting.

Jack Frost hit the television screen in 1992 and became a huge success, with 43 episodes over fifteen series. The story goes that it was David Jason who instigated the series, having read a Frost novel on holiday which impressed him. However, Wingfield was not a big fan of Jason as Frost, feeling that the dark humour in his books was softened by someone with a reputation for comedy, and apparently he only watched the pilot episode, not the rest, unhappy with details such as the absence of the chain smoking that featured in the books. Additionally, in an interview in the *Radio Times* on the 23rd August 1996, he said "my fear is that if I were to watch him, then my next Frost would become him." He also said that he "used to work with a chap called Jack Frost, but he wasn't anything like him." Did Wingfield model the Frost location, Denton, on Basildon? It is quite possible.

Meanwhile, at home in Basildon, Wingfield became the main carer for his invalid wife, Phyllis, and kept out of the limelight. He lived quietly, at three different addresses in Basildon over the years with many neighbours unaware of who he was, and did not attend literary events or parties, declining to appear on television's *Super Sleuths* (ITV 2006) and avoiding the paparazzi. His son, Philip, inherited his own interest in photography, however. (Thanks to Ken Porter, Basildon Borough Heritage, for this information).

Tributes were widely paid upon his death from prostate cancer in 2007. Wingfield had not broadcast his diagnosis five years earlier, continuing to care for his invalid wife until her death in 2004 after 52 years of marriage. Ralph Spurrier (of online bookshop Post Mortem Books) said that "Posterity will, in my opinion and that of many others, including other authors, place him among the greats of the crime-writing world." Fellow crime writer Stuart MacBride said: 'His death is a terrible loss to everyone who loves brilliantly written crime fiction. Rodney's plots were twisted, layered and interwoven; his characters flawed, funny and human; his sense of pace and dialogue second to none. If I can ever manage to be even a third as good a writer as he was I'll consider myself to be very lucky indeed. He'll be sorely missed.' (funeral-notices.co.uk)

Mike Ripley, again, had an interesting anecdote in regard to Wingfield's funeral. "The officiating priest had just informed the congregation that Rodney had insisted on being buried with his mobile phone, just in case of oversights. Right on cue, with immaculate timing, a mobile phone began to ring and everyone in the church held their breath. It turned out to be the priest's own mobile which he'd forgotten to turn off!   As we left the church to the strains of Frank Sinatra singing *My Way* (another specific request from the departed), I was pretty sure I could hear Rodney chuckling somewhere."

Four more Frost books were produced after Wingfield's death, with family approval. *First Frost* was produced in 2011 under the pseudonym of James Henry followed by *Fatal Frost, Morning Frost* and *Frost at Midnight*, with others planned.

VIOLET WINSPEAR 1928 – 1989

Born in Hackney, East London, Violet Winspear grew up to be a legend in the romance community. But while Mills & Boon is in the Oxford Dictionary defined as "romantic story books" its writers are very rarely household names, and Violet was one of these. To go back to where it all started, however...

Her mother was widowed when Violet was four years old and, in common with her peers, Violet left school at 14 and worked in an artificial flower factory alongside her mother, both earning six pounds per week. They lived in a council block on the seventh floor, so not the most auspicious of beginnings. As Bernard McElwaine wrote in the

Sunday Mirror on the 7th August, 1970, "the only way she could make a better world for herself was by creating it in words."

This better world was some years away, because it was 1961 when her first romance novel was sold to Mills and Boon, *Lucifer's Angel*. She had bought her first typewriter with a Christmas bonus from the artificial flower factory, but said (as quoted in the *Sunday Mirror*) "When I started my first novel I had so much to learn - and the library told me all about foreign parts, menus, what the world outside Hackney was like." This first book was about Hollywood, a place she had never visited, but had researched. The publisher initially posted it back and told her to take out a reference to divorce because "people in romantic novels didn't divorce." So she "snipped out the divorce and they accepted it." There were no more divorces in her books. "Just virgins in humble circumstances falling in love with men being a bit devilish."

She was able to become a full time writer just two years later, in between caring for her elderly mother, and a few years later moved to Leigh-on-Sea, on the Southend border. Bernard McElwaine's article describes her as an "old maid" living in a "tiny semi-detached next to a coal merchant's, looking out on a line of washing and large mountains of uncovered coke" when she "lifted her eyes from her typewriter". [Coke had a very different meaning at the time ...] She had managed to escape from London's East End to a fantasy world "in which men with names like Kurt woo girls with names like Moira or Siran". She told McElwaine that she had just sent off her latest book (the 25th). This was *The Castle of the Seven Lilacs*, set in Austria, a place she had only visited via the library.

By 1970, she was earning £5,000 per annum (*Reading Evening Post* 22nd October 1970), the equivalent of nearly £90,000 in 2022. Violet was leading a different life to the one she had experienced as a child. She even appeared on television in August 1970 to discuss her imaginative worlds in a BBC2 programme called – in a parody of romantic novelists' dialogue – *Oh, God, Nigel, I Can't Stand It Any More.*

Various sources quote Violet as aiming to "provide escape and entertainment" and she was certainly appreciated not just by her readers but by Mills and Boon, who asked her in 1973 to launch their new brand: Harlequin Presents, a more sexually explicit range. This was partly because she was one of their most popular and prolific writers, but perhaps also because of the publicity she had created in 1970 when she had been quoted as saying that her heroes should be seen as "capable of rape". Generally speaking, her heroes – in 70 Mills and Boon novels and in serialised romances such as those printed in *Woman's Weekly* in the 1970s – were lean, sardonic, tigerish, rich, in need of love, and cynical only on the surface, fascinating alpha males if a little frightening at times. She also contributed to twelve graphic novels, with one of these novels (*Blue Jasmine*) being turned into a musical in 1983. While she had her critics who felt her storylines were uninspiring or her heroes too controlling, reviews of her books were more likely to carry such adjectives as brilliant or spellbinding.

She never married, never travelled outside of England in spite of her exotic locations (including Morocco, the Caribbean, and the Cote d'Azur) and is unlikely to have ever met an Arab sheikh or a Brazilian playboy, but she obviously felt comfortable writing about them. Her last novel, in 1987, was *A Silken Barbarity*, her final sheikh romance. Her own passion appears to have been for writing, and this she passed on to her nephew, Jonathan Winspear, who also established himself as a writer, particularly of local history and folklore.

Violet succumbed to cancer in January 1989 while still resident in Leigh. According to the *Southend Echo* of 16th January 1989, "Leigh's own Barbara Cartland" had died after a "long fight", with writing "a wonderful therapy" as she battled through chemotherapy. Nearly twenty years later, the Marketing Director of Mills and Boon, Clare Somerville, wrote about her legacy in *The Times* (10th February 2008). She described Violet's "sheikh novel, *Tawny Sands*" as setting "the whole of British womanhood a-tremble" in 1970, regarding Violet as having what it took to write "torrid, sexy romances". Here is a tiny, quintessential sample from *Tawny Sands*:

"He was Raul Cesar Bey [the grandson and heir of a Moorish princess] and the further they travelled into the desert, the more aware she was of his affinity with the savage sun and tawny sands."

As Karen Robinson wrote in that *Times* article – "not even the combined effects of feminism, celebrity culture, chick lit, falling literacy rates, ladette culture and the run-down state of our libraries have put a dent in the female reader's appetite for a good dollop of romance." So thank you Violet Winspear.

WILLIAM WINSTANLEY 1628? – 1698

A true Essex member of the literati, Winstanley was born, lived and died in the village of Quendon, near Saffron Walden. He grew up with his seven siblings in a farmhouse called Berries, moving to Creepmouse Alley in Saffron Walden after marrying Martha, who bore him two children. It was some time before he had any work published, however. In 1655, his *The Muses Cabinet, Stored with Variety of Poems* appeared, with one poem dedicated to Martha, who died in January 1653. (*Oxford Dictionary of National Biography*).

Winstanley re-married the same year and, on the death of his mother in 1670, moved back to Berries, which he had inherited. In the meantime he had written *England's Worthies: Select Lives of the most Eminent Persons* and a number of biographies, focusing on royalist martyrs and political figures. As a staunch royalist during the time of Cromwell, he was one of many who risked life and liberty by objecting to a "reign" which effectively banned the celebration of Christmas.

During Cromwell's years as Lord Protector, however, Winstanley continued to churn out book after book – writing about merchant tailors, about Essex and rural life, about Essex worthies and Essex poets. Hardly any women appear in his books – not unusual at the time of course, leading to accusations of misogyny.

In the 1660s he used the pseudonym of Poor Robin, the name behind very popular almanacs, which sold thousands year on year. Other works by "Poor Robin" were much more light-hearted than works under his own name, e.g. *The Delectable History of Poor Robin the Merry Sadler of Walden (1680)* compared to *The Loyall Martyrology (1665)*. He was also still writing poetry, e.g. *Poor Robin's Perambulation from Saffron Walden to London performed this Month of July 1678*, a doggerel poem dealing largely with the alehouses on the road. (pennyspoetry.fandom.com)

Although the monarchy was restored in 1660 when Charles II was returned to the throne, Winstanley was concerned that there was no immediate return to Christmas celebrations and he was worried that the annual celebration would die out. (See *William Winstanley, The Man who saved Christmas* by Alison Barnes.) For years he lobbied friends in high places to give the poor something to look forward to in the winter, and in his almanacs there were details of his own celebrations – the feasting, the use of local greenery to decorate his home, dancing, story-telling and carol singing. His efforts seemed to pay off and paved the way for Charles Dickens and Queen Victoria to continue to build on his groundwork more than a century later.

Winstanley's second wife died in 1691, and he followed seven years later, with both of them buried in Quendon. A prolific writer with strong views and a strong sense of humour, Winstanley deserves to be remembered, and celebrated, not just in Essex – just like Christmas.

MARY WOLLSTONECRAFT 1759 – 1797

Born in Spitalfields, London, in 1759, Mary spent only around five of her formative years in Essex, but as she had such a short life, this was quite a high proportion! Her father started out in the family business as a handkerchief weaver, but wanted to better himself socially and live in the country. Knowing nothing about crops or livestock, he tried his luck at farming in a number of different locations, funded by money inherited from his father. One such venture was at Epping in 1763, near the forest which covered a much larger area then than now.

Two years later, the family moved to what was seen as a superior location, taking on a farm near the thriving market town of Barking where her father drowned "his financial failures in the bottle and let his wife and children bear the brunt of his frustration" (the *Barking and Dagenham Post* 26 May 2009). This same article refers to Mary as "taking solace in the nature surrounding her Barking childhood home to escape alcohol-fuelled domestic scenes ... gaining a kind of spiritual consolation from the 'reveries' she later described when looking up into the sky from the flat, uninhabited land that lay before her, between the farm, the land known as Barking Level and the Marshes south of the river."

Things went badly and their capital dwindled, meaning they left the area for a farm near Beverley in Yorkshire in 1768, where she received some local schooling, although surrounded by locals who spoke in an accent Mary could barely understand. In later years, she was known to have re-visited Barking, renewing her acquaintance with the market and the crowded wharf.

A lifestyle change came when her father finally gave up on farming and returned to London in 1774. Mary was fifteen, with increased access to books, lectures and discussion groups. It was enough for her to be able to open a school for girls in 1784 (with her sisters), and then work as a governess two years later when the business failed. Her first book, *Thoughts on the Education of Daughters,* in 1787 argued that poor education and early marriage could ruin a woman's life.

As one of the founding feminist philosophers, she caused considerable controversy with her writing, especially the *Vindication of the Rights of Women* in 1792, the classic feminist tome. Unusually at the time, she earned a living from her writing producing 17 books before her death in 1797 following the birth of her second daughter, from two different fathers. (This daughter, also Mary, went on to marry Percy Bysshe Shelley and write *Frankenstein* and you can see a stache of her letters in, interestingly, the Essex Record Office.)

While not a quintessential Essex Girl, Mary Wollstonecraft certainly made her mark on the county as well as the country and the world, and her life was full of adventure and controversy. She was a trailblazer in philosophy, in politics and in defending equality between the sexes and is remembered not just in Essex for her impetuous and exotic love life but also for her radical and forward thinking brain.

LADY EMMA CAROLINE WOOD 1802 – 1879

This celebration of Essex Authors includes some motivation for older wannabe writers: it's never too late! Here we have someone who was not published until after she was 60, but then produced fourteen novels and several books of poetry, mainly romantically inclined.

Emma was actually born in Portugal, because her parents were there at the time bearing in mind that her father was an Admiral in the Portuguese Navy. After the family returned to the U.K., they settled in Truro until Emma, at 18, became a lady's maid to Queen Caroline (until the Queen died). This position resulted in her meeting her future husband, Rev Sir John Page Wood, a Baronet, who was the Queen's "secretary chaplain". They married in 1820, soon after meeting.

It is in 1832 when Emma and her husband are first recorded in Essex, when he became Vicar of Cressing. By this time, Emma had given birth to eight children, four of whom died in infancy and one being stillborn. Her next five children were all born in Essex, and survived into adulthood, the youngest, Katherine, growing up to be the notorious Kitty O'Shea (as a married woman, Kitty had an affair with Charles Parnell, the "uncrowned King of Ireland" nearly ruining him, and harming Anglo-Irish relations).

During this period, Emma became skilful at painting and illustrated at least one of her poetry books. It seems the family in Cressing led quite a Bohemian lifestyle. Emma was a gifted water-colour artist and musician, a friend of John Constable. Such a large family meant they had had to move out of the "damp vicarage" at Cressing to a more palatial house in 1854 – Rivenhall Place.

This was dilapidated at the time but many improvements turned it into something of a mansion, with visitors including Trollope and Tennyson. Trollope in particular was attracted to the surrounds of Rivenhall Place because he enjoyed a "hard ride to hounds" and "stuck at nothing" in the process. (devon-mitchells.co.uk)

Emma was left a widow in 1866 and this seems to be when she turned to writing novels, bringing in a limited income – mainly because of negative reviews. She used her maiden name and the pen name 'C. Sylvester' for some of her work, and also co-authored a book of poetry with her daughter, Anna, in 1865. Her first novel was published in 1866, *Rosewarne*, and the last in 1879, *Youth on the Prow*. The one book that caused controversy, and therefore presumably better sales, was *Sorrow By The Sea*, which exposed the scandal of baby farms at the time (1868). This was a productive year as it was when she also produced *Sabina,* a novel in three volumes.

Anna, and one of her sisters, another Emma, both of whom grew up in Essex, inherited their mother's love of words. Anna, who had become a friend of Trollope, wrote half a dozen novels under her married name Anna Steele (most famously *Gardenhurst* in 1867), and her sister Emma wrote one novel (*Constance Rivers*, also 1867, under her married name Emma Barrett Leonard but not using her title – 'Lady' – as the wife of a Baronet). The young Emma had a preference for song-writing and apparently wrote hundreds, some using the words of poems such as those by Tennyson.

At some point, the Barrett Leonards had taken the ageing Emma into their home, Belhus Park at Ockendon, and this is where she died in 1879, recorded as being due to "heart trouble." Her daughter Emma and at least one of her sons (Evelyn) was at her bedside. Predictably, Emma (Senior) was buried alongside her husband, Sir John, in Cressing churchyard. Less predictable were her last words: "Put away my paint-box and brushes, I shall not want them again." An obituary in the *Illustrated London News* (20th December 1879) described her as "a woman of rare accomplishment, good sense and warmth of feeling."

Antiquarian booksellers Pickering and Chatto describe Emma's novels as being nautical works and have a few rare editions in stock.

LADY MARY WROTH 1587 – 1651

Born in Kent – though sources vary – Mary was the eldest child (of eleven) of Robert Sidney, Earl of Leicester, and educated by private tutors. She married the future owner of Loughton Hall (once owned by Mary Tudor) in 1604. Her husband, Sir Robert Wroth, became a royal forester and the keeper of Woodford Walk, protecting game and leading royal hunts which included King James on several occasions.

Mary, however, was more interested in literary pursuits and turned the manor house into a centre for Jacobean literary life, not too surprising given that her uncle was Sir Philip Sidney, the famous Elizabethan poet.

Mary's husband died of gangrene in 1614, and their two year old son died in 1616, leaving no heir and leaving Mary with enormous debts. She wrote what is perceived as the first full-length novel by an English woman in 1621, *Urania*, an epic prose romance of some 600,000 words. This was considered scandalous at the time, being a thinly disguised satire on the royal court, scandalising high society.

She also wrote a five-act drama *Love's Victory*, and was the first known woman to write a sequence of more than 80 sonnets, which brought her further fame as the first female to write a sonnet sequence and an early proponent of secular poetry. Her work was praised by such luminaries as Ben Jonson who apparently became part of her social circle.

While she achieved a modicum of literary success in her lifetime, her widowhood was mainly occupied with dealing with her debts. Although there was also the affair with William Herbert, the womanising third Earl of Pembroke, which allegedly produced two children. (*Oxford Dictionary of National Biography*).

By 1643, she was known to be living in Woodford and have died by 1653. Where she died and was buried though is unknown. A lady of some mystery, but one who opened the possibilities for women writers of succeeding generations (poetryfoundation.org).

Loughton Hall remained in the ownership of the Wroth family until 1738 and the street name, Wroths Path, remains in their memory, on the edge of Epping Forest. Loughton Hall itself, a Grade II listed building, is now a residential care home.

AUTHORS WHO DID NOT QUITE MAKE THE ESSEX LIST!!

Oliver Goldsmith Although there is a plaque at Duke's Cottages in Springfield Green, Chelmsford, referring to Goldsmith, there seems no real consensus of opinion that confirms he lived there other than briefly. While various historians mention his ending his days there, he in fact died in London (in 1774, age 45) and is buried there. He did, however, know Earl Nugent of Gosfield in Essex, a fellow Irishman, and stayed there occasionally, but this is the only definitive link to the county (*Oxford Dictionary of National Biography*). It is true that his pastoral poem *The Deserted Village* could be about Springfield, when it was a "sweet smiling village" but it is just as likely to be about Lissoy, in Ireland, a village of his childhood. He does refer to himself "living in Essex" in his book *The History of the Earth and Animated Nature* (in the chapter on "Animals of the Dog Kind") where he mentions a fox hunt, but living for how long, that is the question! As a poet, playwright and author, with such famous works as *The Vicar of Wakefield* and *She Stoops to Conquer* under his belt, it would be a feather in Essex's cap, but he cannot, in all conscience, be included.

Rebecca West

Rebecca West, D.B.E. Born in 1892, the mistress (or one of them) of H.G.Wells moved with their illegitimate son, Anthony, to Leigh on Sea in 1917 to be nearer to the much older Wells. The house was called Southcliffe in Marine Parade, a semi-detached house "covered in woodwork" (see *R. West, A Life* by Victoria Glendinning). Toddler Anthony could enjoy the seaside, and Rebecca could sit on her balcony and hear the gunfire in France, but when the Zeppelins passed by overhead, mother and son decided enough was enough and they went back to London after just two years, hence Rebecca not in main "listing"! She wrote eleven novels, with *Return of the Soldier* (set in the First World War) her most famous, and a number of non fiction books mainly on travel and politics. Made a Dame for services to English Literature, she is another Essex author on the Wills's 1937 Famous Authors cigarette cards (died 1983).

Benjamin Disraeli Disraeli is excluded because, obviously, he was not primarily an author, but also because he did not ever "live" in Essex having been born and died in London (1804-1881). However, he did spend a few years of his education at Higham Hall in Epping Forest (1817-1819) and did stay in Southend for several extended periods in 1833 and 1834 as a guest of Sir Francis Sykes and his wife, Henrietta, to whom Disraeli was apparently attracted. He wrote of Porter's Grange, the Sykes' home, as being "a comfortable residence" where he lived "solely on snipe" in a place with a soft climate and sunny skies. He is also known to have visited Paglesham where he acquired a taste for their oysters. Disraeli's epic poem, *Revolutionary Epick*, was apparently partly written at Porter's. It was finished by 1834 when he moved back to London after finding time to hunt in the countryside then around Southend with its "thick woods ... creeks and marshes ... and unusual archipelago of islands."

He had already produced several books before staying in Essex, and wrote another two novels (*Henrietta Temple* - note reference to Henrietta - and *Venetia*) upon returning to London. The more political *Coningsby* and *Sybil* (among others) were completed after he became Prime Minister in 1841, the first to be born Jewish. According to the *Journal of British Studies* (October 1989) Disraeli was a novelist who wanted to be a "great politician".

After four decades in the House of Commons, he was accorded the title of Earl of Beaconsfield, and it is, of course, his role as Prime minister (twice), parliamentarian and political statesman which renders him significant rather than his literary output. His patronage of Porters was particularly flattering given the instrumental role he played in the establishment of the modern Conservative Party.

POETIC LICENCE

There are a number of well known poets who spent time in Essex, but they are not included in the main body of this book, because we are mainly talking about short stays – for a variety of reasons. But they are just too famous to ignore!

Alfred Lord Tennyson lived at Beech Hill House, High Beach at Epping between 1837 and 1840, having been born in Lincolnshire in 1809. At Epping he completed several poems and part of *In Memoriam* including references to the bells of nearby Waltham Abbey: "Ring out, wild bells". He was twenty-eight on arrival, newly engaged, but his biographers describe this period as his "silent and morose decade." Tennyson befriended Dr Allen, who ran a nearby asylum whose patients then included the poet John Clare.

An unwise investment in Dr Allen's ecclesiastical wood-carving enterprise soon led to the loss of much of the family fortune, and led to his marriage being postponed and a bout of serious depression. He wrote to his fiancée, Emily, describing his outlook in Epping Forest as a "muddy pond" although on the other hand he seems to have enjoyed skating there when it was frozen. (*Epping Forest* by William Addison, 1945.)

Things changed during the 1840s when he started earning real money for his work. He became Poet Laureate in 1850 and was still writing until his death at age 83 in 1892.

John Clare wrote over 2,000 poems in his lifetime, and, in the 1820s was treated as a prodigy (he was born in 1793). A decade later, sales of his poetry were in decline as his expenses increased (he had seven children) and he was forced to take part time work as an agricultural labourer. His creditors were hovering, his mental health deteriorating, and he felt unable to support himself or his family, so his publisher recommended him to spend time with Dr Allen at High Beach in Epping. Allen had humane and enlightened views and was a pioneer in modern methods of healing, having opened his "asylum" in 1825.

In *Epping Forest: Its Literary and Historical Associations*, William Addison refers to John Clare as the "peasant poet" who spent four years in Dr Allen's care. Here he was apparently encouraged to write and enjoy walks in the forest, and he wrote to his wife of his beautiful surroundings. He was there at a similar time to Tennyson, and the two must have met. But Clare was missing his home and family so much that he walked out in 1841 aiming to walk to his home in Northamptonshire, described in his sequence of poems: *Journey Out of Essex*.

Five months after arriving home he was committed to Northampton General Lunatic Asylum, his confused state of mind having become too difficult for his wife to handle. This is where he died in 1864. It was his wife, his other loves and nature which were his greatest influences although his most famous, epic, poem, *Child Harold*, was directly influenced by Byron's *Childe Harold's Pilgrimage*. (*Oxford Dictionary of National Biography*.)

Edward Thomas, who became known as one of the War Poets, was writing poetry before the First World War, waxing lyrical about the English countryside although a Londoner. When he joined the Artists' Rifles' Officer Training School in 1915, he was based at Hare Hall in Romford and wrote a number of poems there including *The Chalk Pit*, supposedly inspired by the chalk cliffs of nearby Purfleet. Other Essex place-names feature in his poetry, e.g. Havering-atte-Bower in *Myfanwy*. His first posting was to High Beach at Epping in huts temporarily erected, with his wife and children living nearby. He later returned to Hare Hall to instruct officers, and in the ten months there he wrote over forty poems. In 1916 he was commissioned into the Royal Artillery and was killed at Arras on Easter Monday 1917, aged just 39. (*Front Line Essex* by Michael Foley, 2005.)

George Granville Barker spent very little time in Essex. However, as he was born in Loughton in 1913, he merits a blue plaque on his birthplace although the family moved to Fulham, London, when he was just six months old. T.S.Eliot regarded him as a genius, and he composed poetry until his death in 1991, including *Sonnet to My Mother*, and *Calamiterror* (inspired by the Spanish Civil War). Barker's poetry featured in many 20th century collections, and he had over 20 volumes of poetry published. This was a man who liked a drink, who liked a quarrel, who fathered 15 children by four women, who wrote extensively about sex and led a controversial and bohemian life. A character too colourful to exclude.

Sarah Martin was born in 1768 with little known of her childhood, which was probably in Devon, the place where she had family and where she finished off a traditional three line rhyme (when in her 30s) by adding on material about her sister's household. This comic rhyme about Mother Hubbard became popular, not easy in a time of poor communication, and ended up being published in 1805 as *The Comic Adventures of old Mother Hubbard and her Dog.* The publishers claimed that this sold 10,000 copies in a few months (bl.uk)! At some point she settled in Loughton because she was buried there, a single woman, in St Nicholas Church, in 1826, where other members of her family lie. Interestingly, some sources (e.g. Jonathan Gash in his novel *Faces in The Pool*) affirm that she caught the attention of Prince William Henry as a young seventeen-year old but, as a rector's daughter, was ruled out as an unsuitable partner, leaving Sarah lovelorn.

Sarah Flower Adams, born in Harlow in 1805, became an actress after marrying in 1834 and moving to Loughton after a spell in London. However, her health did not allow her to continue in that profession and she turned to composing lyrics for hymns such as *Nearer My God to Thee*, her most famous (of thirteen) because it was allegedly played as the Titanic sunk. Her small poetry output, mainly religious and political, was topped by *Viva Perpetua*, a dramatic – and popular – epic poem she wrote in 1841 about the sufferings of the early Christians. Sarah and her sister, Eliza, certainly moved in literary circles and were friends of Robert Browning. Both sisters, however, died of consumption, Sarah having cared for Eliza during her final weeks but succumbing herself in 1848. She is buried in the Foster Street cemetery near Harlow, with a blue plaque remaining at her Loughton home. (Her husband, William Bridges Adams, an engineer, wrote a couple of non-fiction books about transport.) "Poetic Licence" allows Sarah space here although hers was definitely not a short Essex stay.

ESSEX LINKS TO CLASSICAL LITERATURE

Charles Dickens

Barnaby Rudge features 'The Maypole Inn' which is apparently based on the 17th century 'King's Head' in Chigwell, with its name taken from the 'Maypole' pub also in Chigwell. Dickens obviously visited the area, because he is quoted as describing it as "the greatest place in the world" with a "delicious old inn opposite the church … [and] … beautiful forest scenery" (in a letter to his friend John Forster.)

Pickwick Papers refers to a coach at the 'Black Boy' in Chelmsford taking Toby Weller and Alfred Jingle to Ipswich. According to Robin Marchal, M.A. (essex.ac.uk) Dickens himself stayed at the 'Black Boy' in 1835. There is, interestingly, a Quilp Drive, Dombey Close and Magwitch Close in Chelmsford! *Great Expectations* has references to Sluice House, which seems to be modelled on the 'Lobster Smack' on Canvey Island, with its smuggling history and proximity to the prison hulks of the 19th century. The convict Magwitch, in chapter 42, says that he grew up in Essex "thieving turnips for a living".

Christmas Stories included *Mugby Junction*, based on Tilbury Riverside. (Note: Dickens gave readings as part of a tour at Colchester in 1861 and at the defunct Laurie Hall in Romford.)

Bram Stoker

Dracula's Essex house, Carfax, is apparently based on Purfleet House, with its own chapel; built by Samuel Whitbread, the brewer, in 1791 and now the site of St Stephen's Church. The area could have been visited by Stoker when he was working in London at The Lyceum.

William Shakespeare

Midsummer Night's Dream was written for the marriage of Sir Thomas Heneage, who lived at Copped Hall near Loughton. It was first performed in the long gallery in 1594.

Richard II mentions Pleshey as the residence of the murdered Gloucester's widow, with its "empty lodgings and unfurnished walls".

The Merry Wives of Windsor, according to legend, was performed by the legendary Nell Gwyn and other court favourites, at New Hall, Boreham, a mansion with a vast hall.

Cymbeline is loosely based on Cunobelinus, a Celtic King of ancient Britain who made Colchester (i.e. Camolodunum) his capital in the eponymous play.

P.S. An early conspiracy theory suggests that some (or many?!) of Shakespeare's works were written by Edward de Vere of Hedingham Castle who wrote poems and plays for Queen Elizabeth I and was patron of an acting company.

Jane Austen

In *Emma* the heroine talks of Southend-on-Sea at a time it was establishing itself as a spa town. "I must beg you not to talk of the sea. It makes me envious and miserable; I who have never seen it! South End is prohibited, if you please." Mrs Knightley springs to the defence of the resort saying that she "never found the least inconvenience from the mud."

Arthur Ransome

The backwaters of Walton, Hamford Water, which form part of the Essex marshes, were the setting for Arthur Ransome's 1930 book *Secret Water*. He changed the names of some of the network of the marshland islands, i.e. from Horsey Island to Swallow Island, from Skippers to Mastodon, and from Honey to Bridget. This was the eighth in the famous *Swallows and Amazons* series and was voted the most popular book featuring Essex at the 2023 Essex Book Festival. The seventh in the series, *We Didn't Mean To Go To Sea*, features Harwich. Ransome himself was known to have sailed the Hamford Water area in his yacht the *Nancy Blackett*.

George Orwell

In *Nineteen Eighty-Four,* Colchester was the town he chose to be obliterated by an atomic bomb. Also, according to sources such as the *Romford Recorder* (11th July 2020), *Down and Out in Paris and London* features Romford in disguise as Romton, with its workhouse and its humiliating treatment of the destitute based on Orwell's experience there in the 1920s when he deliberately became a vagrant for the purposes of research!

Paul Gallico

Although an American novelist, Gallico set his most famous story, *The Snow Goose,* in the desolate Essex marshes. Set in the 1930s and published in 1941, it is still in print and still popular.

MORE LITERARY CONNECTIONS TO ESSEX

Rodney Ackland This playwright, born in 1908, was as popular in his day (i.e. the 1930s particularly) as Noel Coward and Terence Rattigan. He was born in Westcliff-on-Sea and spent his childhood touring with his mother, a musical comedy star, which partly explains why he studied at London's Central School of Speech Training and Dramatic Art. After this he has proved problematic to trace – the assumption would be that he lived in London because his work was aimed at West End theatre, with his first play *Improper People* staged there when he was just 21. He also did some directing and acting but his main success was in writing scripts for stage and for film, being regarded at one point as the British Chekhov. Of his 19 plays, the most famous is probably *Call for Arms!* (1940), and, of his ten films, perhaps *49th Parallel* (1949, starring Laurence Olivier). Although he died in Surrey in 1991, his *Absolute Hell* was still drawing in audiences at the National Theatre in London in 2018.

Una Silberrad was born in Buckhurst Hill (1872) with her first novel published at age 27: *The Enchantress*. Another 39 "middlebrow" (conservative) novels followed, featuring strong women, one of whom impersonated a man and became Prime Minister (*The Affairs of John Bolsover*, 1907). In 1932, aged 60, she moved with her younger sister to Wick House in Burnham on Crouch. Her last book was published in 1944, a year after her sister (her typist!) died. Una's possibly mediocre output ended following a stroke in 1955. (*Essex Journal* Autumn 2009)

Frank Pepper, the original creator of *Roy of the Rovers*, was born in Ilford in 1910, and, after completing the first four instalments, had a long career writing for a huge range of comic "heroes" including *Dan Dare* instalments for *The Eagle*. Upon retiring, he moved to Cornwall where he died in 1988. (britishcomics.fandom.com)

John Alec Baker may have only had one success but is included because of its unique content. He was educated at King Edward VI Grammar School in Chelmsford, an area which prompted his interest in walking, cycling and nature. He spent most of his life (1926-1987) in the area and gave up his job with the Automobile Association to focus on writing – in the 1960s – with *The Peregrine* (1967) winning the Duff Cooper Memorial Prize for its innovative depiction of nature. Website maldon.nub.news paints a fascinating picture of a myopic, reserved man who used poetic descriptions such as the "Essex landscape on acid," his book based on his observations of peregrine falcons through the seasons in Great Baddow, West Hanningfield and Heybridge.

Reginald Blyth ring a bell? Perhaps not. From Ilford, this man, born in 1898, was educated at Ilford County High School, the son of a railway clerk. However, he was imprisoned during the First World War because of his stance as a conscientious objector, but earned a First Class degree in literature at the University of London after the war and left to teach English to students at the Imperial University in Seoul, Korea, in 1924. His students included Korean royalty. Following the Japanese attack on Pearl Harbour, Blyth was interned as a British enemy alien. He managed to finish his first book *Zen in English Literature and Oriental Classics* while in the camp in Kobe. As a writer with a Japanese wife (his second marriage), Blyth produced many articles on Asian culture and literature, and became particularly interested in haiku poetry and was at the forefront of its popularisation in the 1950s. He wrote around twenty books on Zen and Haiku and other forms of Japanese and Asian literature, dying in Tokyo in 1964, far away from home. (alchetron.com)

Sarah Smith Better known as the author Hesba Stretton, Sarah was born in Shropshire in 1832, starting her journalistic career at 26 with regular contributions to Charles Dickens' *Household Words,* with several based on family experiences. Other stories appeared in such publications as *The Argosy* and *Chambers' Journal.* From 1863, after moving to Manchester, Sarah wrote a number of children's books, her most successful being *Jessica's First Prayer* in 1866 which raised awareness of the plight of street children, which sold over 2,000,000 copies in her lifetime, was translated into fifteen languages, as well as into Braille, and was followed up with *Jessica's Mother* two years later. Twenty more children's books, highlighting slum poverty and abuse, followed, plus serials for such publications as *Cassell's Family Magazine.* Sarah also wrote some adult novels, mainly about female vulnerability – she herself never married. During these years, the family moved around, living in London and briefly in Europe. By 1870 Sarah and her sister Elizabeth had arrived in Loughton in Essex, but how long did they stay is the question! This was when Sarah lobbied to establish the Society for the Prevention of Cruelty to Children, alongside Benjamin Waugh. By 1892, however, the sisters had settled in Ham, Richmond, in what the *Oxford Dictionary of National Biography* describes as their first permanent home. Elizabeth died in 1811, and Sarah eight months later (in October). A *Sunday at Home* obituary praised her 'long, happy, useful and noble life' but whether Essex can lay claim to her is a mystery.

Rev. Philip Morant contributed a book which has proved invaluable for local historians ever since. This was his *The History and Antiquities of the County of Essex* published in instalments between 1763 and 1768, over fifteen years after he had produced his *The History and Antiquities of Colchester.* Although born in Jersey in 1700, he took up his first curacy in 1722 at Great Waltham and moved to other rectories around Essex while writing his histories, splitting his latter years between Aldham and Colchester. He died three years after his wife, after nearly thirty years of marriage (in 1770) and is laid to rest beside her at St Margaret's Church, Aldham. (*Oxford Dictionary of National Biography.*) The church boasts a stained glass window in his memory, and his profile is on the village sign, with the Philip Morant School in Colchester another reminder of his Essex associations and the significance of his two principal works.

Samuel Purchas was an even earlier Essex cleric who turned his hand to writing about travel, hopefully inspiring overseas expansion and enterprise, and his collections (compiled in *Purchas his Pilgrimes*) were read and admired latterly by such luminaries as Samuel Taylor Coleridge (Britannica.com). He was born in 1577 in Thaxted (died 1626) and built on the work of "the father of modern geographers" Richard Hakluyt who had published his own book *Divers[e] Voyagers* in 1582.

CONCLUSION

My look at *Famous Essex Authors You Have Never Heard Of* has come to an end, and I hope you will agree that they are an inspiring, fascinating bunch who deserve to be remembered and appreciated. While some have produced books which have become films and television programmes, all have had to struggle to make it into print for various reasons – timing, their gender, their finances, familial opposition, self-doubt, their unpopular views, their social status, even their own mental health in some cases.

While their treatment has been, to some extent, subjective, I have tried to be fair in my summation and to that end I have stuck to the facts rather than to trying to analyse either the authors or their books. Each author could be the subject of a book to themselves, but this list should show potential writers, especially those from Essex, that there is no formulaic type that can produce good work. I hope that the interest and enthusiasm of all the authors featured shines through.

While I have focused, for practical reasons, on authors who are no longer with us, it would have been wonderful to have met some of them, but, sadly, I never did, even those who were around in my lifetime. Imagine a dinner party with any six of these people – what stories, what anecdotes, what creativity!

They have not all been easy to research, but, with help from local museums, archivists, historians, the British Library and the British Newspaper Archive, it has been possible to reveal each individual's journey, to bring their stories to life, stories that could otherwise stay hidden. I have always been just as interested in people as I am in places.

It has been a joy to unearth so many interesting writers, especially so many with working class backgrounds, but if I have missed anyone at all (I hope not!), then do let me know. What I do hope is that I have proved that Essex is not all about TOWIE or blondes with stilettos, or lager louts at the seaside. It is eclectic, poetic, diverse, entertaining and educated. It is proud, and I am proud to be one of its champions.

Dee Gordon is an adopted Essex girl, having started life in the East End of London. Although widely published in teenage magazines when working as a teenage secretary, she did not return to this, her first love, until selling her recruitment business in 2000. Since then she has written nineteen local history books and a couple of novels as well as the occasional poem.

She has been living in the Southend area since 1983, a place she aspired to after many day trips from the East End in the 1950s. Her late husband and autistic son have not appreciated her efforts, considering them "such a lot of work." But she considers that the work has been fun, interesting and worthwhile, and she has learnt a lot about her adopted county!

Her most successful books, in terms of sales, have also been the ones she has most enjoyed researching, i.e. *Southend Memories* (about the heyday of the city in the 1950s and 1960s), *The Little Book of the East End* (trivia about the area where she was brought up), and *Infamous Essex Women* (revelations about famous women associated with Essex). She thoroughly enjoyed studying for her belated B.A.Hons. in English Literature with the Open University and is a member of the Society of Women Writers and Journalists, contributing to magazines such as *Essex Life*, *Best of British*, *This England* and *Who Do You Think You Are?* See www.deegordon-writer.com for more information.

Other Titles available from
Essex Hundred Publications

THE RISE, FALL AND RISE OF HORSE RACING IN CHELMSFORD
FULL CIRCLE By David Dunford
In the 18th and 19th centuries Chelmsford Races, held on Galleywood Common, were the most eagerly anticipated event in the Essex social calendar. They had something for everyone: the aristocracy could flaunt their wealth and power, the working classes enjoyed a rare day off and crooks and conmen fleeced the unwary.
ISBN 9781739931612

BUFFALO'S BILL'S WILD WEST
by David Dunford
The First Reality Show in Essex revealing the extraordinary story of Buffalo Bill, his Wild West show and what happened when they came to Essex in the early 1900s.
ISBN 9780993108389

MILTON, CHALKWELL AND THE CROWSTONE
by Marion Pearce
Milton hamlet has sunk into oblivion, but still to be found are traces of the 'middle town' between Leigh-on-Sea and Southchurch. Chalkwell is a thriving residential area which has its roots in the large estates of Victorian era and the Crowstone has been a landmark in the Thames estuary for nearly eight hundred years.
ISBN 9781739931605

THE RIDDLE OF BOUDICA
Explores the 'facts' of the rebellion as far is known and examines the resultant heritage, legacy and mythology which has grown up around it.
ISBN 9780993108334

ONCE UPON A TIME IN SOUTHEND (AND DISTRICT)
Cartoons are one of the most popular staples of newspapers. The cartoonists' genius lies not just with drawing skills but their ability to bring together contemporary and historical events in a single image.
ISBN 9780993108396

BATTLEFIELD ESSEX
2000 years of conflict in Essex
ISBN 9780993108341

THE ESSEX HUNDRED HISTORIES
From the Roman sacking of Colchester to Ford's modern day wind turbines each chapter reflects the diversity of the county as well as showing the role Essex has played in the nation's development.
ISBN: 9780993108310

MAGNA CARTA IN ESSEX
Essex barons were at the forefront of those who pushed hard for the Magna Carta, with Robert Fitzwalter, Lord of Dunmow appointed their leader. Yet within three months of the charter being sealed England was at war and Essex racked by conflict.
ISBN 9780993108303 £7.99

THEY DID THEIR DUTY, ESSEX FARM
Never Forgotten
A book that tells the story of Essex Farm, a First World War cemetery in Belgium, that will forever bear the county name.
ISBN 9780955229596

THE NUMBERS HAD TO TALLY
by Kazimierz Szmauz
A World War II Extraordinary Tale of Survival
ISBN: 9780955229572

DIGITAL EDITIONS AVAILABLE

Essex Farm
The Numbers Had to Tally
L33 and other stories from WWI

Essex Hundred Publications publishes a range of Essex centered local history books. By Essex we mean not just the county of Essex as it is today but also the areas of Essex that have been absorbed into London since 1965.

The company also distributes a range of local history books from other publishers and has a large portfolio of Essex images.

Essex Hundred authors are also happy to give talks on the subjects published.

For further details check out www.essex100.com
or e-mail ask@essex100.com

Essex Hundred Publications

Books written, designed and printed in Essex.
Available from bookshops, book wholesalers,
direct from the publisher or
online www.essex100.com